For Sophie.

Text Copyright © Yola Thorp 2023
Illustrations Copyright © Ayesha King 2023

Library of Congress Control Number 2023917443
ISBN 978-1-7366263-9-9 (hardcover)

Printed in the United States

All rights reserved. No part of this publication may be reproduced, stored, or transmitted in any form or by any means (including electronic, mechanical, photocopying, recording, or otherwise) without prior written permission from the publisher.

Our books may be purchased in bulk for promotional, educational, or business use. For more information please contact us at info@SightSeeingPress.com or find us on the web at www.SightSeeingPress.com.

First Edition

Sightseeing Sophie in

Sophie's heart raced with excitement as the train pulled into the station, announcing their arrival in the city of Boston. The towering buildings seemed to whisper tales of history and adventure, calling out to her curious spirit.

"This sign has watched over the city for decades," her mom uttered, pointing at the prominent Paramount sign towering above them.

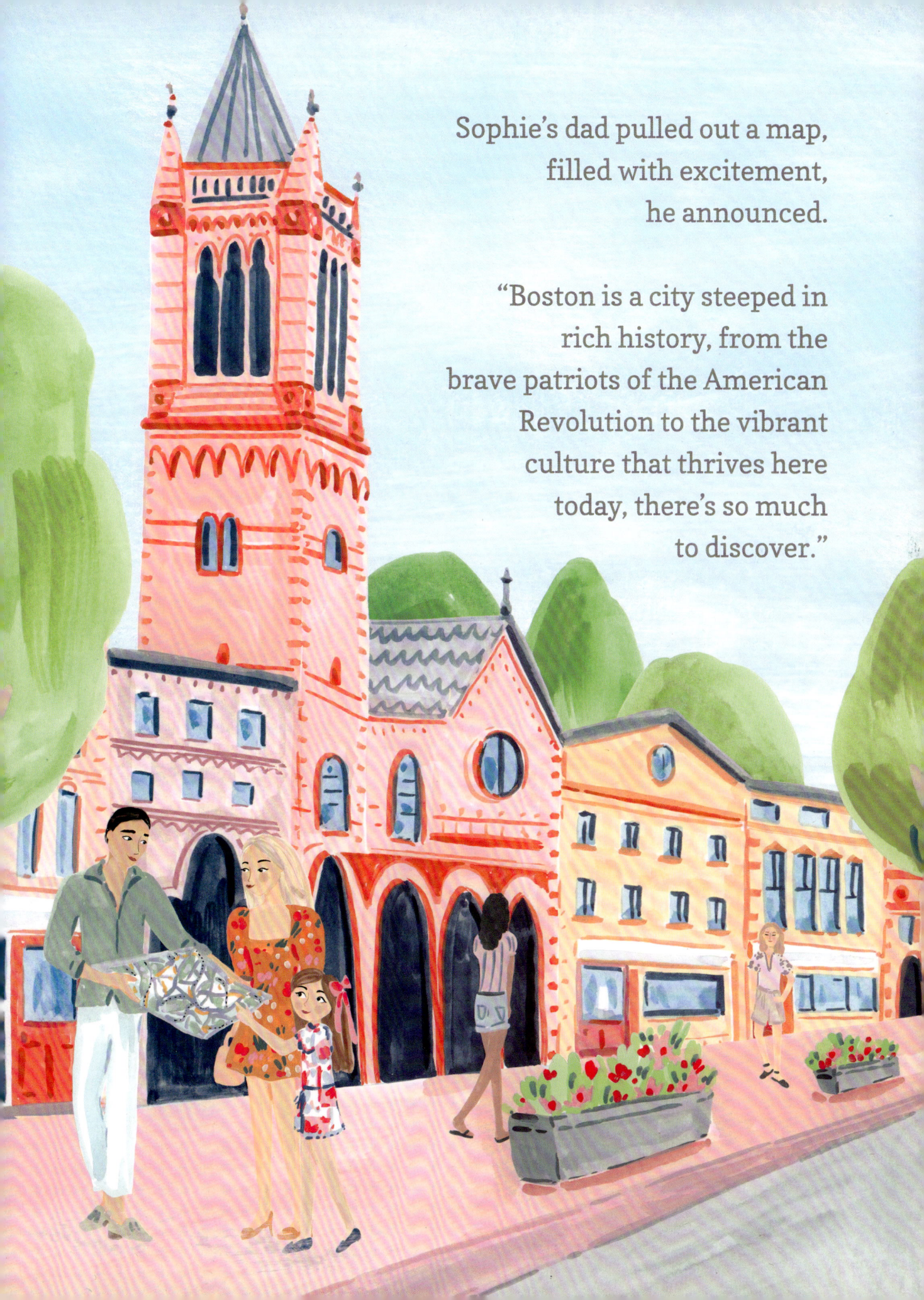

Sophie's dad pulled out a map, filled with excitement, he announced.

"Boston is a city steeped in rich history, from the brave patriots of the American Revolution to the vibrant culture that thrives here today, there's so much to discover."

The winding paths of the Public Garden opened up to a world of colorful flowers and tall, rustling trees. A statue of George Washington, one of the founding fathers, stood tall, seemingly watching their every move.

"Look, Sophie! The Swan Boats have been a beloved tradition here for over a century. They're like something out of a fairy tale!" Sophie's mom explained, pointing to the iconic boats gliding across the water.

Eager to delve deeper into Boston's history, Sophie's family embarked on a journey along the famous Freedom Trail.

The 2.5-mile-long path marked by a line of red bricks wound its way through the city, leading them to significant sites that played a pivotal role in the birth of a nation.

"Did you know darling, that one of the heroes who walked these very streets was Paul Revere?" - her mother asked.

"At the dawn of the American Revolution, he embarked on a daring midnight ride, warning fellow colonists of the approaching British troops."

"This trail is a tribute to the resilience and spirit of the American people and allows us to walk in the footsteps of those who fought for liberty." her dad added.

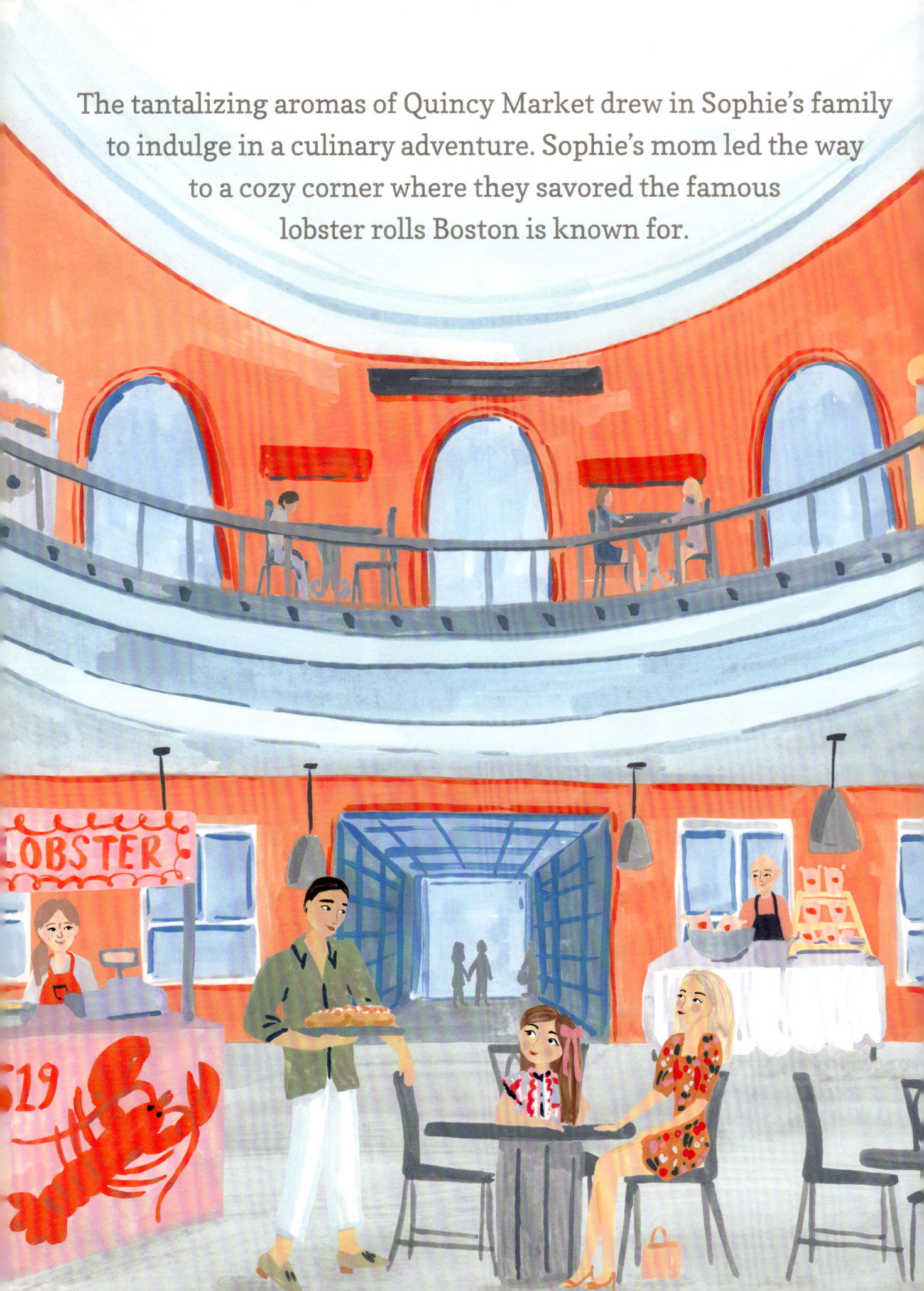
The tantalizing aromas of Quincy Market drew in Sophie's family to indulge in a culinary adventure. Sophie's mom led the way to a cozy corner where they savored the famous lobster rolls Boston is known for.

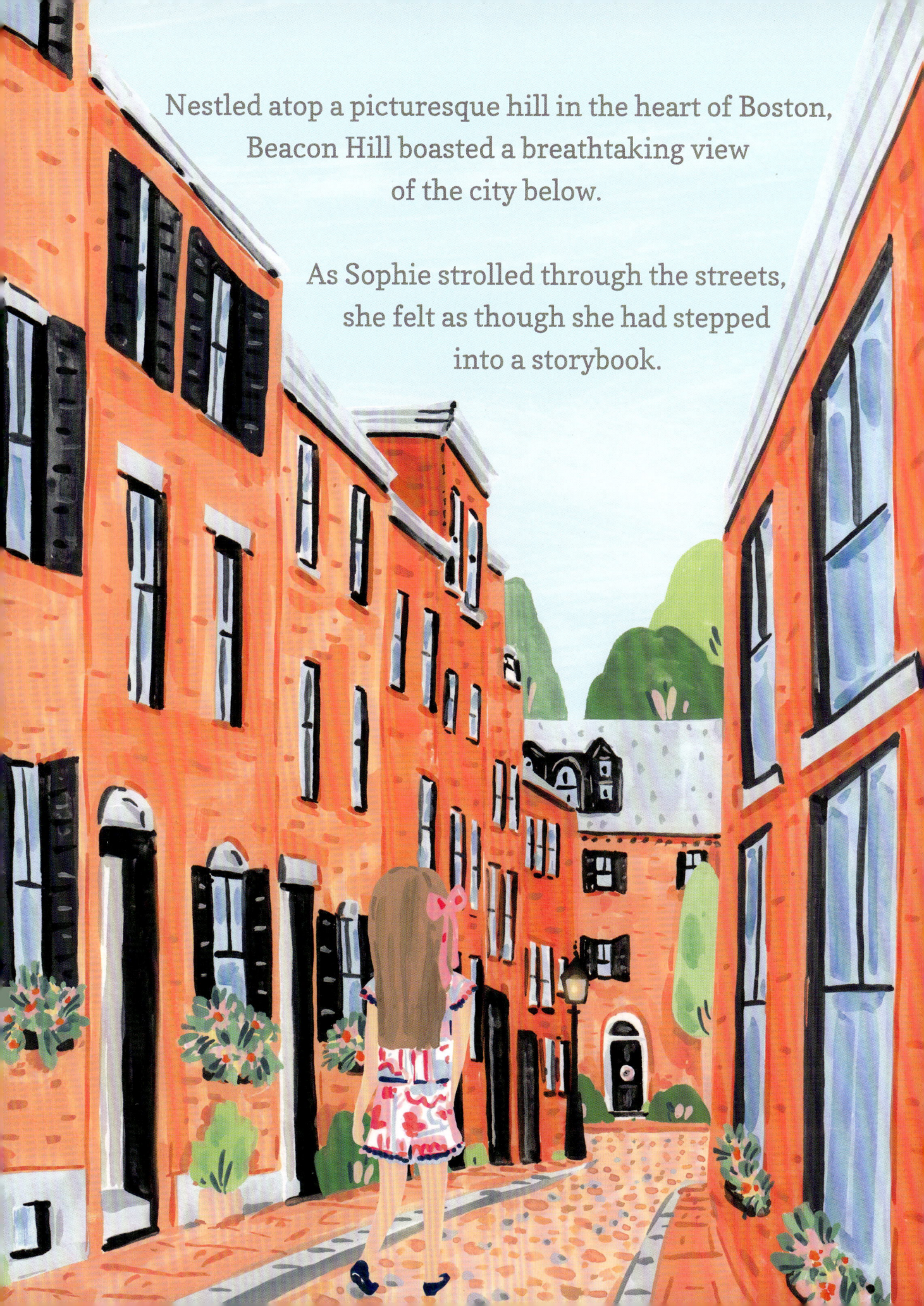

Nestled atop a picturesque hill in the heart of Boston, Beacon Hill boasted a breathtaking view of the city below.

As Sophie strolled through the streets, she felt as though she had stepped into a storybook.

"We've arrived at Boston Common, the oldest public park in the country!" her dad shared.

Sophie's eyes widened with excitement as she took in the stunning view and glimpsed the shiny gold dome of the State House.

A short while later, they made their way to Newbury Street, Boston's shopping hub, filled with trendy boutiques and inviting cafes. Her gaze naturally drifted to the Prudential Tower, a sleek contrast to Newbury Street's historic charm.

Sophie beamed in delight upon the sight of tall, gleaming buildings reaching for the sky, their glass windows catching the sunlight.

The streets were transformed into a canvas for modern, colorful art installations, creating a unique atmosphere.

The Seaport District felt like a different world from the historic parts of Boston they had explored earlier.

"All this walking is making me hungry." Sophie remarked as the aroma of freshly baked bread and simmering sauces filled the air along the streets of Boston's North End, also known as "Little Italy."

They settled into a cozy trattoria, where checkered tablecloths and the joyful chatter of families set the scene.

"Today let's visit the Isabella Stewart Gardner Museum!" Sophie's mom suggested the next morning.

"It was founded in 1903 by Isabella Stewart Gardner, a remarkable art enthusiast and collector, who carefully acquired over 7,500 incredible artworks."

Boston
UNITED STATES OF AMERICA

PORTER SQUARE

CHARLESTOWN

BELMONT

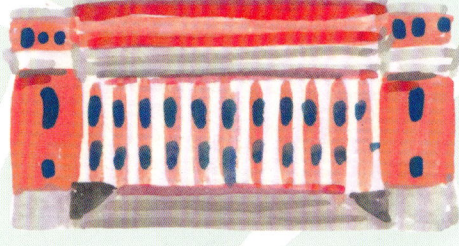

HARVARD

FREEDOM TRAIL

CHARLES RIVER

FENWAY

ISABELLA STEWART GARDENER MUSEUM

BOSTON PUBLIC GARDEN

BRIGHTON

CHESTNUT HILL

WOODLAND HEATH

Stepping into the museum, Sophie and her family were greeted by the sight of an Italian style courtyard.

Throughout the museum paintings by famous artists like Rembrandt, Vermeer, and Botticelli hung on the walls.

The Charles River flowed gently through Boston, offering a serene view.

Sophie took in the tranquil atmosphere as she indulged in a heavenly bite of the iconic Boston cream pie, relishing the velvety custard and the luscious chocolate topping.

Stepping on the hallowed grounds of Harvard University in Cambridge, Sophie and her family were surrounded by centuries of academic prestige.

"I bet you girls didn't know that Harvard was founded in 1636 and is the oldest university in the United States?" Sophie's dad asked.

"We sure did! It's also one of the most prestigious universities in the world, consistently ranking among the top schools. Its faculty and alumni have made groundbreaking discoveries, won Nobel Prizes, and shaped the world in countless fields." her mom chimed in.

Excitement filled the air as Sophie and her family entered the historic Fenway Park, home of the beloved Boston Red Sox. As they settled in their seats, surrounded by a sea of passionate fans,

Sophie's mom shared some fascinating facts, "Fenway Park is one of the oldest baseball stadiums in the country? It's been standing here since 1912, witnessing incredible moments in baseball history."

The next morning, Sophie's eyes sparkled with anticipation as they embarked on the ferry bound for the picturesque island of Nantucket.

The island greeted them with its quaint cobblestone streets, charming cottages adorned with colorful hydrangeas, and the inviting scent of the sea.

At the historic Nantucket Whaling Museum, they delved into the island's rich maritime history and marveled at the massive skeleton of a whale. They learned about the daring voyages of Nantucket whalers who braved the open seas in pursuit of these magnificent creatures.

Sankaty Head Lighthouse stood tall and proud against the backdrop of the Atlantic Ocean.

Sophie imagined the lighthouse keepers of the past diligently tending to the light, guiding ships safely through treacherous waters.

In the afternoon, they decided to embark on a sailing adventure. The gentle breeze filled their sails, propelling them forward. With each passing moment, the vibrant hues of the sky painted a breathtaking backdrop for their journey.

The next moring, Sophie woke up to the soft glow of the sun filtering through her window. The rhythmic sound of seagulls and the distant crash of waves filled the air.

She eagerly hopped out of bed, knowing that a day of exploration awaited her.

Pedaling through the cobblestone streets of Nantucket, Sophie and her parents embarked on a bike ride. The wind tousled their hair as they explored the island's charming neighborhoods and coastal paths.

The air smelled like freshly brewed coffee, and a hint of salty sea breeze tickled their noses from the nearby harbor. The sound of laughter and music was everywhere as street performers entertained passersby on Main Street.

As their time on Nantucket drew to a close, Sophie and her parents felt captivated by the natural beauty, maritime history, and inviting charm of this island.

Nantucket had given her a glimpse into a world untouched by the fast pace of modern life—a world where the rhythm of the ocean dictated the ebb and flow of each day and Sophie felt a sense of tranquility wash over her as she bid farewell to the island.

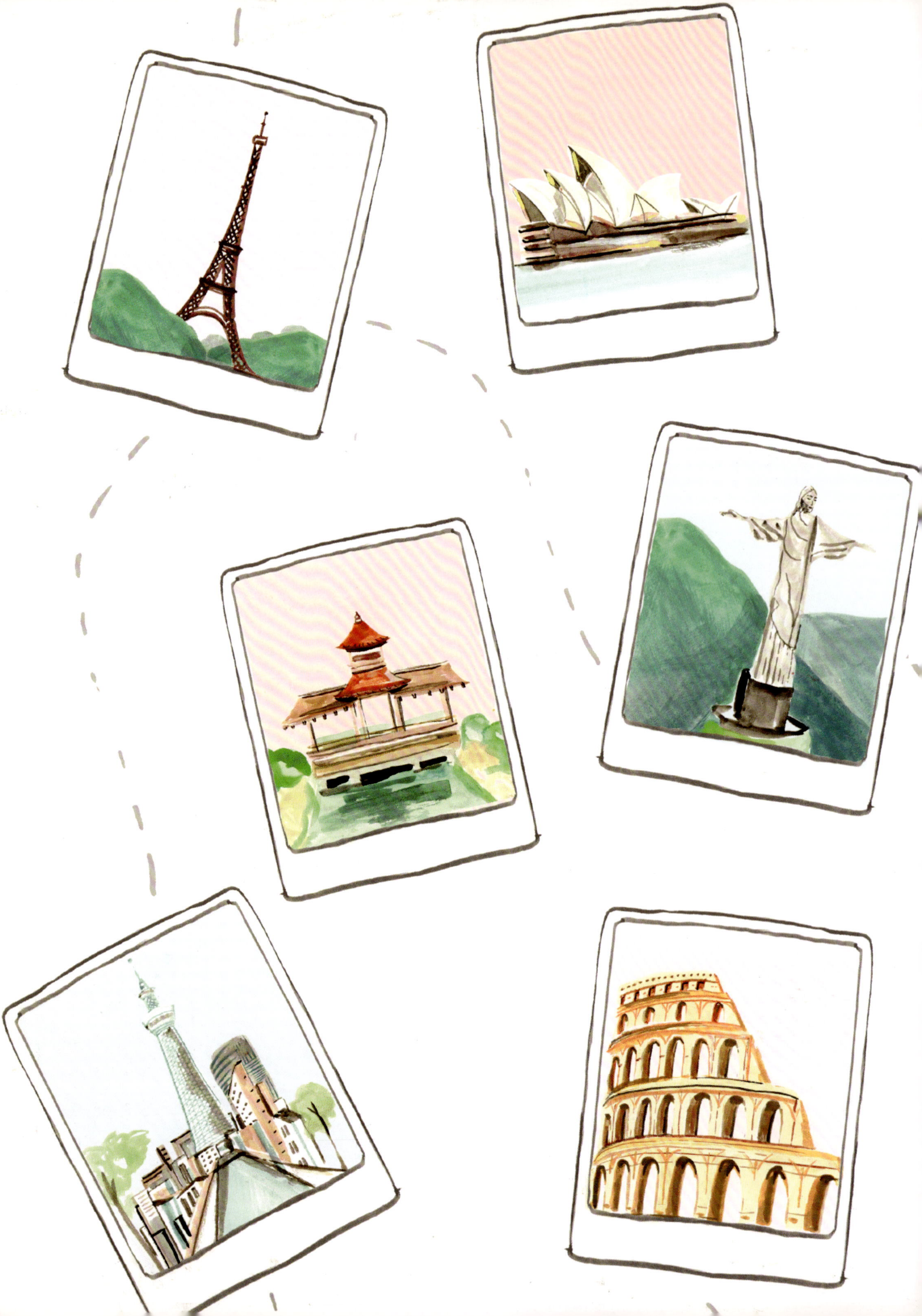

Healthy Heart, Healthy Brain

The Best Foods for Peak Cardiac and Cognitive Health

2025 Report

A Special Report published by
the editors of *Tufts Health & Nutrition Letter*
in cooperation with The Friedman School of Nutrition Science and Policy
Tufts University

Cover image: © kali9; fcafotodigital; Carol Yepes | Getty Images

Healthy Heart, Healthy Brain: The Best Foods for Peak Cardiac and Cognitive Health

Consulting Editor: Grace Giles, PhD, Lecturer, Psychology, Tufts University. Adjunct Lecturer, Friedman School of Nutrition Science and Policy, Tufts University

Author: David A. Fryxell
Creative Director, Belvoir Media Group: Judi Crouse
Editor, Belvoir Media Group: Cindy Foley
Production: Mary Francis McGavic

Publisher, Belvoir Media Group: Timothy H. Cole
Executive Editor, Book Division, Belvoir Media Group: Lynn Russo

Print ISBN 978-1-941937-87-7
Digital ISBN 978-1-941937-88-4

To order additional copies of this report or for customer-service questions, call 877-300-0253 or write: Health Special Reports, 535 Connecticut Avenue, Norwalk, CT 06854-1713. To subscribe to the Tufts monthly newsletter, *Health & Nutrition Letter*, call 800-274-7581 or write to the address above.

This publication is intended to provide readers with accurate and timely medical news and information. It is not intended to give personal medical advice, which should be obtained directly from a physician. We regret that we cannot respond to individual inquiries about personal health matters.

Express written permission is required to reproduce, in any manner, the contents of this publication, either in full or in part. For more information, write to Permissions, Belvoir Media Group, 535 Connecticut Avenue, Norwalk, CT 06854-1713.

© 2025 Belvoir Media Group, LLC

FROM THE CONSULTING EDITOR

Grace Giles, PhD
Lecturer, Psychology, Tufts University. Adjunct Lecturer, Friedman School of Nutrition Science and Policy, Tufts University

Eating right is not a new idea. It dates back hundreds, if not thousands, of years. The concept of what constitutes a healthy diet has changed, however, and it continues to change—almost every day. This Special Health Report is designed to guide you through the constantly evolving science of proper nutrition. We help you wade through the often-confusing sea of advice from popular media and explain what nutritionists and medical doctors say about what to eat and what to limit.

Nutrition is important for both your heart and your brain health, with research increasingly demonstrating that these major physical powerhouses require similar sources of fuel. Many of the same nutrients benefit the heart, the vascular system, and your brain. So, when you adopt a heart-healthy diet, you are also feeding your brain what it requires to function effectively.

According to a study published in JAMA Neurology, more than one in three cases of Alzheimer's disease and related dementia were associated with modifiable risk factors, including:

- midlife obesity
- midlife hypertension
- physical inactivity
- depression
- smoking
- diabetes

Many of these risk factors are related to cardiovascular disease, and three of them—obesity, hypertension, and diabetes—are key to heart health as well.

This is only the beginning of the ways in which scientists are discovering connections between what you eat and drink and how your brain ages. Experts estimate that we have learned more about the human brain in the last decade than in all the previous centuries. So, this scientific adventure is just beginning, as never before has so much science been focused on exploring the secrets of the brain.

This Special Health Report explains healthy dietary patterns for your heart and brain, with specific foods and nutrients that are important for such a diet. You will read the latest research (marked as "New Findings") that has advanced our understanding of how lifestyle affects the heart and brain. This Special Health Report offers information on the changes you can make to your diet—such as swapping out foods high in saturated fats (e.g., butter, red meat) for those rich in unsaturated fats (e.g., olive oil, nuts, fish)—that may help you improve your heart and brain health. As you will see, eating right for your heart and brain is easy and delicious.

The proliferation of misinformation, along with the popularity of dietary fads, means it's especially important to keep up with the real science that's pointing the way toward protecting your heart and keeping your brain youthful. This Special Health Report will show you how emerging science can be put to work in your own daily life.

At Tufts University's Friedman School of Nutrition Science and Policy, we are always exploring ways simple changes in your daily life can improve your cardiovascular health and reduce your risk of cognitive decline and dementia. You can't change your genetic makeup or your age, but you can change your diet and lifestyle—and we're here to help you.

Grace E Giles

Grace Giles, PhD

TABLE OF CONTENTS

FROM THE CONSULTING EDITOR 3

NEW FINDINGS 5

1 HEART HEALTH AND BRAIN POWER 6
Healthy Body, Healthy Mind 6
Understanding Heart Disease 7
Cognition and the Brain 7
Vascular Risk Factors 9
Reduce Your Risks 11

2 PROTECTING HEART AND BRAIN 12
Steps to Health 12
Blood Vessels and Cognition 13
Cerebrovascular System 13
Hypertension and the Brain 13
DASH vs. Hypertension 14
Pounds and the Brain 15
Diabetes and Dementia 15
Diet Makes a Difference 16
Controlling Cholesterol 17
Reducing Triglycerides 18
Diet and Diabetes Risk 18
Managing Your Weight 18

3 PATTERNS THAT PROTECT 19
Mediterranean-Style Eating 19
Med + DASH = MIND Diet 21
NU-AGE for Brain Health 23
Nutrient-Dense Patterns 23
Picking Your Pattern 23

4 MACRONUTRIENTS FOR HEART AND BRAIN 24
Understanding Carbs 24
Fresh Thinking on Fats 26
Protein Fads and Facts 29
Science and Common Sense 29

5 BRAIN FOODS 30
Nutritious Nuts 31
Berries for the Brain 32
Eat Your Veggies 33
Omega-3s from the Sea 34
Dark Chocolate Findings 35

6 HEALTHY BEVERAGE CHOICES 36
Yes, Coffee Counts 37
Tea: Drinking Plants 38
Coffee and Tea Brain Benefits 39
Packaged Beverages 39
Updates on Alcohol 40

7 NUTRIENTS FOR HEART AND BRAIN 42
Plant Power 43
Exploring Antioxidants 44
Carotenoids for Cognition 45
Fish-Oil Pills 46
The B Vitamin Puzzle 47
Seeking Vitamin D Benefits 48
Vitamin E and Alzheimer's 49
News on Multivitamins 50
Nutrient Essentials 50

8 THE FACTS ON "BRAIN BOOST" PILLS 51
Understanding Supplements 52
Ginkgo Biloba 53
Green-Tea Powder 53
Ginseng and Grape Seed Extract 54
Turmeric/Curcumin 54
Creatine for Mental Muscles 55
Nootropics 56
Mood Supplements 57
Buyer Beware 58

9 HEART-BRAIN LIFESTYLE SECRETS 59
Activity vs. Aging 60
How Exercise Helps 61
Getting Going 63
Healthy Sleep Habits 64
How to Stick to Healthy Habits 64

10 AN ACTION PLAN FOR A HEALTHY LIFESTYLE 67
Numbers You Should Know 68

RECIPES 71

OTHER MEAL IDEAS 77

GLOSSARY 78

RESOURCES 80

New Findings

- Six Keys to Heart Protection 8
- Glucose Levels Linked to Post-Stroke Risk 10
- Weighing BMI Usefulness 11
- Control Blood Pressure Now for Brain Benefits 14
- Diabetes Management Lowers Dementia Risk 16
- Cholesterol Role in Dementia Complicated 18
- Dietary Choices Cut Cognitive Risk 18
- Diet, Lifestyle Add to Cognitive Reserve 20
- Mediterranean Cardiovascular Risk Reduction 21
- Introducing the "Atlantic Diet" 22
- Weight Loss Matches MIND 23
- The Brain Benefits of Whole Grains 26
- Olive Oil Proves Protective 27
- Varied Diet Better for the Brain 31
- Too Much Thiamine Linked to Decline 47
- Low Vitamin D Linked to Alzheimer's Risk 49
- Brain Protection from Multivitamins 50
- Memory Supplements Evidence Mixed 52
- Neuriva Shows Promise 56
- Active Adults Average Bigger Brains 61
- Sedentary Behavior Linked to Dementia 62
- Mental Stimulation May Protect Brain 63

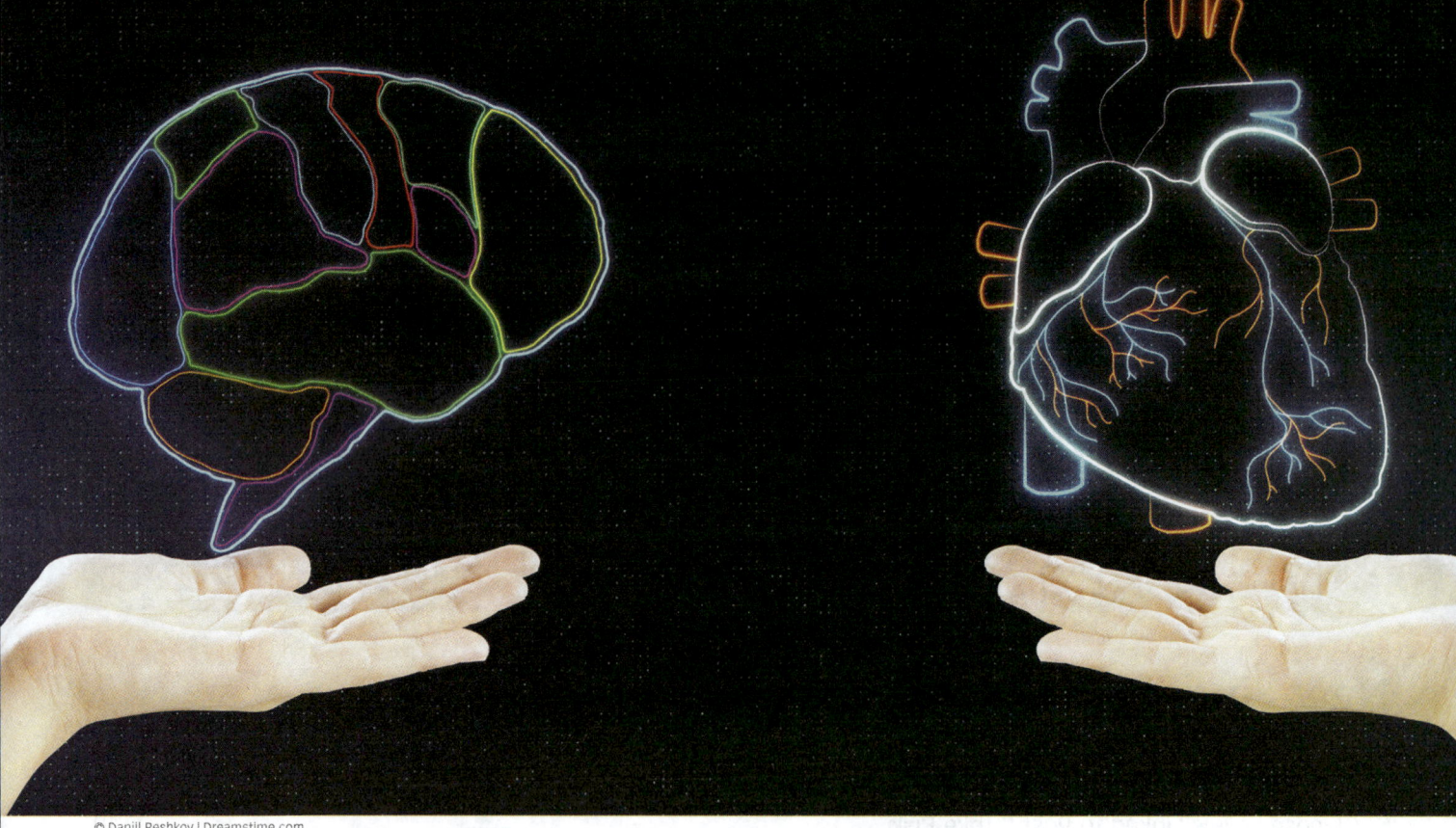

Your heart and brain require an abundance of fuel—the right fuel—to do their jobs in keeping your body functioning at a healthy level.

1 Heart Health and Brain Power

The heart and the brain have different critical functions, but they depend on each other. Your brain controls your heart rate. Your heart delivers the oxygen and nutrients your brain cells need. Although an average brain makes up only about 2 percent of total body weight, your brain uses 20 percent to 25 percent of the blood supply circulated by your heart. When your brain is hard at work, it requires an even greater blood supply to do its job.

Connecting the heart to the brain and the rest of the body is a network of veins and arteries called the vascular system. Keeping your vascular system healthy helps protect the health of your heart and your brain.

Healthy Body, Healthy Mind

It's not surprising, then, that maintaining a healthy cardiovascular system is important for protecting against dementia and other brain issues. A study in *Neurology* in July 2022 found that the most important risk factors for dementia vary with age—but all relate to cardiovascular health. Scientists used data on almost 5,000 people from ages 55 to 80 from the long-running Framingham Heart Study and its offshoots. At age 55, diabetes and high blood pressure (hypertension) were the most significant predictors of eventual dementia. Ten years later, cardiovascular disease was most strongly linked to developing dementia. At age 80, diabetes and blood pressure again topped the risk factors, along with stroke history.

A related study, published in January 2023 in *Alzheimer's & Dementia*, reported that abnormal cholesterol and glucose (blood sugar) levels as early as age 35 may be associated with Alzheimer's disease risk later in life. Such associations had previously been observed only in adults ages 55 and older. Lower HDL ("good") cholesterol and higher triglyceride levels measured in early adulthood and high blood glucose levels in middle adulthood contributed to future risk of developing Alzheimer's.

The good news is that, even if Alzheimer's runs in your family, you can benefit from heart-healthy foods and lifestyle choices. In another study published in July 2022 in *Neurology*, researchers followed the habits and cognitive health of 11,500 people for over 25 years. Participants were scored on the American Heart Association (AHA) "Life's Simple 7" of physical activity, diet, obesity, smoking, blood pressure, cholesterol, and blood sugar (now updated to include sleep for "Life's Essential 8"). During the study, over 2,200 cases of incident dementia were noted. Healthier scores at midlife were associated with lower dementia risk for participants with all levels of genetic risk.

Shared Risks

Coronary heart disease is the No. 1 cause of death, according to the AHA "Heart Disease and Stroke Statistics," but diseases of the brain—especially Alzheimer's disease and other dementias—are catching up. According to the AHA, global dementia increased by more than 144 percent and deaths increased by more than 184 percent between 1999 and 2020.

When the heart isn't healthy, the brain can suffer. A study published by the American College of Cardiology in March 2022 showed that about one in three survivors of a heart attack had notable mental decline in the months following the attack, including memory loss or not being able to recognize a loved one. The cognitive impairment was temporary in only about half the cases.

Diseases of the heart and brain are associated with many of the same risk factors, including high blood pressure, obesity, type 2 diabetes, and smoking. Addressing these risk factors is good for the heart and the brain because it keeps the vascular system healthy. While exercise is the most important lifestyle factor for heart-brain health, the evidence that healthy dietary choices can help protect your aging brain continues to add up.

In a 2022 study published in the *American Journal of Clinical Nutrition*, for example, women with higher-quality diets were at lower risk of cognitive decline. Researchers followed almost 50,000 female nurses for 30 years, comparing self-reported cognitive decline with adherence to several diet-quality scores. Healthy dietary patterns included the Alternate Mediterranean Diet (AMED), Dietary Approaches to Stop Hypertension (DASH), and Alternate Healthy Eating Index 2010 (AHEI-2010). The healthiest diets were associated with a lower risk of severe cognitive decline, with risk reductions ranging from 19 percent to 43 percent. Participants who improved their diets over time also saw a reduction in the risk of severe decline (see "Six Keys to Heart Protection" on the next page).

Understanding Heart Disease

Cardiovascular disease is a general term that refers to diseases of the heart and blood vessels. Some heart issues are ones you were born with, and some involve problems with the heart muscle (such as heart failure) or electrical system (arrhythmias like atrial fibrillation). But the most common type of heart disease is coronary artery disease (CAD).

CAD is caused by atherosclerosis, which is the buildup of fatty deposits (plaque) in the blood vessels. Over time, plaque makes arteries less flexible, which is why atherosclerosis is called "hardening of the arteries." The plaque causes arteries to narrow or become blocked. Plaque in the arteries supplying blood to the brain can lead to a stroke. With CAD, atherosclerosis can lead to chest pain (angina) from reduced blood flow to the heart. Plaques can rupture and block a coronary artery, which causes a heart attack.

Cognition and the Brain

Your brain is responsible for everything, including your heartbeat, breathing, sleep, body temperature, movement,

---

Life's Essential 8

The American Heart Association's Life's Essential 8 is a guide of eight simple steps to cardiovascular health:

1. **Eat better.** Aim for an overall healthy eating pattern that includes whole foods, lots of fruits and vegetables, lean protein, nuts, seeds, and cooking in non-tropical oils such as olive and canola.
2. **Be more active.** Adults should get at least 150 minutes of moderate or 75 minutes of vigorous physical activity per week.
3. **Quit tobacco.**
4. **Get healthy sleep.** Most adults need seven to nine hours of sleep each night.
5. **Manage weight.**
6. **Control cholesterol.** High levels of non-HDL, or "bad," cholesterol can lead to heart disease.
7. **Manage blood sugar.**
8. **Manage blood pressure.** Levels less than 120/80 millimeters of mercury (mmHg) are optimal. High blood pressure is defined as over 130 mmHg systolic pressure (the top number in a reading) or over 80 mmHg diastolic pressure (bottom number).

Note how many of these factors can be affected by your diet: weight, cholesterol, blood sugar, and blood pressure.

NEW FINDING

Six Keys to Heart Protection

A healthy diet is associated with a healthier heart and vascular system, according to a global study of almost 150,000 people in 21 countries. Researchers scored diets based on consumption of six foods associated with health benefits: fruit, vegetables, nuts, legumes, fish, and whole-fat dairy. During an average follow-up of 9.3 years, those consuming the greatest amounts of these foods had a 30 percent lower mortality risk compared to those with the lowest diet scores. Higher intakes of healthy foods were associated with a lower likelihood of heart attack and stroke. An analysis of five additional studies from 70 countries produced similar results.

European Heart Journal, July 3, 2023

Signs of Dementia

Symptoms of dementia vary but typically include:
- Challenges in planning or solving problems
- Changes in mood or personality
- Confusion with time or place
- Decreased or poor judgment
- Difficulty completing familiar tasks
- Memory loss that disrupts daily life
- Misplacing things and losing the ability to retrace steps
- New problems in speaking or writing
- Trouble understanding visual images and spatial relationships
- Withdrawal from work or social activities

Source: Alzheimer's Association

---

memory, perception, learning, problem-solving, communication, decision-making, judgment, and emotion. If something goes wrong in the brain, it impacts one of these functions.

Changes that affect thinking and memory impact what's known as cognition. Changes in cognition can be caused by an underactive thyroid (hypothyroidism), severe vitamin B_{12} deficiency, high stress, depression, sleep disturbances, and exposure to toxins. Symptoms can usually be reversed when these conditions are properly treated. Changes in thinking, memory, behavior, or motor skills also can be caused by cancer and concussion or traumatic brain injury, but the two main things that can go wrong in the brain are dementia and stroke.

Mild Cognitive Impairment

Often the earliest sign of dementia is "mild cognitive impairment" (MCI), a stage between normal forgetfulness due to aging and more serious cognitive decline. MCI manifests as problems with thinking and memory that do not interfere with everyday activities. People with this condition often are aware that they are showing signs of impairment. Not everyone who develops MCI progresses to Alzheimer's or other dementia, however.

Symptoms of MCI include:
- Difficulty performing more than one task at a time
- Inability to solve problems or make decisions
- Forgetting recent events or conversations
- Taking longer to perform difficult mental activities

Dementia

One in three people is likely to have some form of dementia by age 85. Dementia refers to a decline in a person's memory and other cognitive abilities that interferes with normal daily life.

Dementia is not normal aging. Many conditions can cause progressive cognitive decline, including dementia with Lewy bodies, frontotemporal dementia, and Parkinson's disease. But the most common cause of dementia, accounting for between 60 percent and 80 percent of all cases, is Alzheimer's disease.

Alzheimer's disease. Every year, about a half-million Americans develop Alzheimer's disease, and that prevalence is increasing. An estimated 6.5 million Americans older than 65 have Alzheimer's—a figure expected to almost double by 2050.

Two types of damaging brain formations, called plaque and tangles, are characteristic of Alzheimer's disease. Plaque is formed by a protein, beta-amyloid, which comes from fatty membranes that surround nerve cells. When pieces of this "sticky" protein clump together, they form plaques.

Tangles affect another protein, called "tau." In a healthy brain, parallel strands of tau proteins function like highways, carrying essential nutrients. In people with Alzheimer's, tangles of collapsed tau block the orderly flow of nutrients to the brain, much like traffic jams. Eventually, the cells deprived of nutrients die.

Typically, plaques and tangles strike first in areas important for learning, memory, thinking, and planning. As they spread through the brain, Alzheimer's disease worsens.

Vascular dementia. The second-most common cause of dementia is vascular dementia. If atherosclerosis narrows the arteries leading to the brain, the flow of nutrients and oxygen can be reduced and blood pressure can rise, causing damage to large or small vessels in the brain. Even Alzheimer's dementia has a known vascular component.

This vascular component explains why conditions that impact heart health—including heart disease, diabetes, stroke, high blood pressure, and high cholesterol—are associated with a greater risk for dementia.

While results from human trials examining vascular dementia risk reduction have been mixed, an older study published in The Lancet in 2015 showed promise: The two-year randomized controlled trial from Finland found that at-risk older adults receiving vascular risk monitoring and interventions around diet, exercise, and cognitive training were less likely to have changes in cognition than a control group receiving general health advice.

Stroke

According to the AHA, in 2020, stroke accounted for one of every 21 deaths in the United States. Most strokes result from vascular disease. Ischemic strokes, which account for 87 percent of all strokes, are caused by a blockage within an artery that supplies blood to the brain or in the brain itself. This cuts off blood flow to the part of the brain fed by the blocked vessel, causing brain cells to die. There are two forms of blockages:

▸ **A blood clot that develops in an artery within the brain** (called a thrombus).
▸ **A blood clot that develops somewhere else in the body,** breaks loose and travels in the bloodstream to the brain, where it blocks a smaller blood vessel (called a cerebral embolism).

If a blood vessel is blocked temporarily, it causes a transient ischemic attack (TIA), called a "mini stroke." Mini strokes may occur repeatedly, leading to noticeable cognitive damage over time. They also are risk factors for a full stroke.

The second major type of stroke is a hemorrhagic stroke. It occurs when a weakened blood vessel in the brain ruptures and begins bleeding. The blood can damage the surrounding brain tissue.

According to the Stroke Awareness Foundation, there are over 7 million stroke survivors in the United States, two-thirds of whom are disabled. Unfortunately, about 25 percent of people who recover from their first stroke will have another within five years.

Vascular Risk Factors

Genetics and age are two risk factors for atherosclerosis and other vascular diseases you cannot control, but you can make a difference in other risk factors, often by making healthier lifestyle choices. These risk factors, outlined in the following sections, are also linked to the development of dementia.

High Blood Pressure

High blood pressure (hypertension) is a leading risk factor for heart attack and stroke. The increased pressure of blood pushing against the artery walls makes them more vulnerable to damage, such as rupture. These damaged areas provide an ideal environment for plaque to accumulate. Eventually, hypertension may damage the heart itself.

High blood pressure also affects the brain. Researchers found that hypertension is associated with greater damage to the brain's white matter, which insulates and protects the neural circuits. This disrupts activity in brain neurons and impairs brain function.

Healthy lifestyle choices, however, can reduce your risks even when you're diagnosed with high blood pressure, according to a February 2022 study in *JAMA Network Open*. The study, which followed over 14,000 individuals in China with hypertension for up to 10 years, found that improvements in lifestyle after a hypertension diagnosis were associated with significantly lower risk of death. Lifestyle factors included diet, physical activity, sleep duration, smoking status, and body mass index.

High Cholesterol

High cholesterol, or hyperlipidemia, is a well-known contributor to an increased

---

Alternatives to Dementia Diagnosis

Many conditions that can cause dementia-like symptoms can sometimes be stopped or even reversed with treatment. According to the National Institutes of Health, these conditions include:

- Side effects of certain medicines
- Emotional problems, such as stress, anxiety, or depression
- Some vitamin deficiencies
- Drinking too much alcohol
- Blood clots, tumors, or infections in the brain
- Delirium, a sudden state of confusion and disorientation
- Head injury, such as a concussion from a fall or accident
- Thyroid, kidney, or liver problems
- Normal pressure hydrocephalus, an abnormal buildup of cerebrospinal fluid in the brain

NEW FINDING

Glucose Levels Linked to Post-Stroke Risk

High blood glucose levels in stroke survivors—who are at greater risk of dementia—are associated with faster cognitive decline, according to an analysis of 982 patients from four population studies. These findings suggest that glucose management in stroke survivors may help preserve cognition after stroke. The data included information on cognitive function before and after stroke, along with post-stroke measures of blood pressure, LDL cholesterol, and glucose. Cognitive function declined over time in all the stroke survivors. However, higher post-stroke glucose levels—but not LDL cholesterol or blood pressure levels—were associated with faster overall cognitive decline. The estimated difference in overall cognitive function between stroke survivors with the highest and lowest glucose levels at 12 years was 5 percent faster. This is roughly equivalent to aging 1.6 years faster for every 10 milligrams per deciliter (mg/dL) increase in glucose levels in stroke survivors.

JAMA Network Open, April 11, 2024

---

risk of heart disease. Cholesterol is a waxy type of fat (lipid) that is transported throughout the body on spherical particles known as lipoproteins (composed of lipids and proteins). Cholesterol is a key component of every cell in your body. Your liver produces all the cholesterol your body needs, but you also get some cholesterol from the foods you eat. Genetics plays a role in how much cholesterol your body makes on its own.

The two main types of cholesterol are:
- **High-density lipoprotein (HDL):** This is often referred to as the "good" cholesterol, since it helps remove cholesterol from your blood and returns it to your liver for removal from the body. High levels of HDL are associated with a lower risk of cardiovascular disease, though recent research suggests this relationship is complex.
- **Low-density lipoprotein (LDL):** This is often called "bad" cholesterol. It's a key component of the arterial plaques that can cause heart attack, stroke and other conditions.

Currentlyh, there is no recommended daily limit for cholesterol intake from food. Instead, limiting saturated fat is believed to be more important than limiting dietary cholesterol intake for controlling blood cholesterol levels. In addition, eating a high-fiber diet, limiting alcohol, and being physically active, can help improve your cholesterol levels.

High Triglycerides

Triglycerides are a fat and part of your lipid panel blood test for cholesterol. High triglycerides may contribute to atherosclerosis. Some triglycerides come from the foods we eat, but others are made in your liver to store extra calories that are not needed right away. Eating more calories than you burn can cause high triglyceride levels in the blood.

The foods that raise triglycerides are most often carbohydrates. Eating refined carbohydrates—food made with white flour and added sugar, like white bread products and desserts—especially contributes to higher triglyceride levels.

People who are overweight are more likely to have high triglycerides or abnormal cholesterol levels. This is known as dyslipidemia. One recent study found that about 60 percent to 70 percent of people with obesity have dyslipidemia.

Diabetes

According to the latest statistics from the Centers for Disease Control and Prevention (CDC), about 11 percent of the U.S. population have diabetes and 38 percent have prediabetes.

Your body breaks down the food you eat into a type of sugar called glucose, which is the primary fuel your cells run on. The pancreas releases insulin, which serves as a sort of "key" that lets that glucose move from your bloodstream into your cells (see "Glucose Levels Linked to Post-Stroke Risk").

Type 2 diabetes, which is preventable, begins when cells don't respond normally to insulin (insulin resistance). The pancreas makes more insulin to try to get cells to respond. Eventually your pancreas can't keep up, and your blood sugar rises. High blood sugar is damaging to the body and can cause other serious health problems, including heart disease.

Heart disease and stroke are the most common causes of death in adults with diabetes. This is because, over time, high blood sugar levels from diabetes can damage blood vessels, nerves that control blood vessels, and the heart.

Diabetes also can harm the brain. Your brain consumes a higher percentage of glucose than any other organ in your body. A growing body of research shows that people with various forms of dementia experience insulin resistance in the brain. Some scientists theorize that, when brain cells stop responding normally to insulin, it can interfere with the ways your brain cells communicate, use energy, and fight infection.

Overweight and Obesity

Excess body weight is associated with cardiovascular disease and other risk factors for heart disease and dementia, including diabetes, inflammation, and high blood pressure. Most physicians use the body mass index scale (BMI) to determine if you are overweight, although this measure is increasingly controversial. According to the Centers for Disease Control and Prevention (CDC), nearly 42 percent of adults ages 20 and over have obesity and 32 percent are overweight.

In one long-running study, being overweight or having obesity at ages 50 or older was associated with an increased risk for developing dementia.

Fortunately, if you are overweight, losing just 5 percent to 10 percent of your body weight may help reduce your risk of dementia. Gradual weight loss can have similar protective effects on the many other conditions associated with obesity (see "Weighing BMI Usefulness").

Belly fat. People can carry excess weight in many different parts of their bodies. Having a high amount of fat around the abdomen, also known as "belly fat," is especially dangerous, and a growing waistline can have a negative effect on both the heart and the brain. Yet not all belly fat is the same.

Visceral belly fat is located around and between the internal organs, such as the stomach, liver, and intestines, while subcutaneous fat lies just beneath the skin. Researchers have discovered that visceral belly fat is more dangerous and can release damaging substances that play a role in the development of both heart disease and Alzheimer's disease.

The combination of high blood pressure, abnormal cholesterol levels, high blood glucose, high triglycerides, and excess body fat around the waist creates metabolic syndrome. People with metabolic syndrome are at an increased risk for both heart attack and stroke.

Reduce Your Risks

Even if you have a family history of cardiovascular disease or dementia, you may not develop either condition. A healthy diet and lifestyle can reduce your chances of developing these conditions, regardless of genetics. Similarly, having no family history of these conditions doesn't guarantee you are at low risk.

Lifestyle interventions are important for all individuals, regardless of other potential risk factors. Research shows that lifestyle modifications may prevent cognitive decline and improve heart health. An in-depth 2020 analysis in *The Lancet* concluded that four in 10 dementia cases worldwide may be preventable by addressing modifiable risk factors.

Even people at higher genetic risk for Alzheimer's disease can benefit from a healthy lifestyle, according to a Chinese study of more than 29,000 older adults followed for over 10 years. The paper was published Jan. 23, 2023, in *BMJ*. Researchers divided participants among three groups based on six healthy lifestyle factors: healthy diet, regular physical exercise, active social contact, active cognitive activity, never or previously smoked, and never drinking alcohol. Those with four to six healthy lifestyle factors saw the slowest cognitive decline, and those with two to three factors declined more slowly than those with one or none. The presence of the apolipoprotein E gene (associated with greater Alzheimer's risk) did not affect the apparent protective benefits of healthy lifestyle choices.

The choices you make today can affect your heart and brain health tomorrow. So let's start learning about how to make those healthy changes.

NEW FINDING

Weighing BMI Usefulness

While body mass index (BMI)—a ratio of weight to height—is a useful public health tool, its ability to predict health risks on an individual level has recently been questioned. An analysis of national health survey data concluded that a BMI in the "overweight" range (22.5 to 29.9) was not associated with a higher risk of death, especially in older adults. The study analyzed data on over 554,000 adults with an average age of 46 years. Being underweight (BMI less than 18.5) or obese (30 or higher) was generally associated with higher risk of death in the nine to 20 years of follow-up. The relationship between overweight and risk of death, however, was inconsistent. The authors concluded that the clinical value of BMI on an individual level has limitations; BMI does not account for differences between sexes and genders, across the life cycle, and, importantly, across racial/ethnic groups. You and your health-care provider should not ignore your BMI, but it should be only one tool of many when determining risk for conditions like cardiovascular disease and type 2 diabetes.

PLoS One, July 5, 2023

No doubt about it. Science shows that living a healthy lifestyle with mental stimulation, physical activity, and low stress helps defend your body from both heart and brain disease.

2 Protecting Heart and Brain

The potential of lifestyle changes to affect heart-brain health has led to some good news: Predictions that rates of Alzheimer's disease and other dementias will explode as the nation's population ages may have been too pessimistic. According to one study, rates of dementia have declined in recent years. Moreover, when people do develop dementia, it is striking at an older age.

Experts on aging credit this encouraging trend to our improved understanding of the brain, coupled with a population better informed about health and nutrition. Evidence shows, for example, that people who take steps to control their blood pressure and cholesterol have a lower incidence of dementia.

A study published in *Alzheimer's & Dementia* in October 2022 suggests that the sooner you start protecting your heart and brain, the better. Signs of cognitive impairment may appear nearly a decade before individuals are diagnosed with dementia, according to the analysis of U.K. Biobank data on more than 5,000 participants, initially ages 40 to 69. Those participants, all of whom subsequently developed dementia or other brain-related conditions such as Parkinson's disease, were compared to nearly 500,000 control subjects.

Steps to Health

We saw last year that midlife cardiovascular conditions may affect women's cognition more than men's. Initially ages 50 to 69, 1,857 participants in the Mayo Clinic Study of Aging were given a battery of mental tests every 15 months, and their medical records were checked for cardiovascular conditions. Most cardiovascular conditions were more strongly associated with cognition among women; coronary heart disease and other cardiovascular conditions were associated with global cognitive decline only in women. In addition, diabetes, high cholesterol, and coronary heart disease were associated with language score declines only in women. However, congestive heart failure was associated with language score decline only in men.

Another risk factor is stroke, which was the fifth leading cause of death overall in 2021, according to the Centers for Disease Control and Prevention. Many more people suffered disabilities from stroke. But deaths and disabilities from Alzheimer's disease and other dementias combined outrank those attributed to strokes. In recognition of this, the American Heart Association's Heart Disease and Stroke Statistics annual report recently added a chapter on brain health.

Blood Vessels and Cognition

Blood vessels supply oxygen and nutrients to the brain, so problems affecting those blood vessels or the heart itself can impair brain health.

If atherosclerosis, or "hardening of the arteries," narrows the arteries leading to the brain, the flow of nutrients and oxygen can be reduced and blood pressure can rise, causing damage to vessels in the brain. This can result in impaired cognitive function.

In addition to the direct brain damage that may be caused by a stroke, victims of stroke who survive are at a greater risk for impaired cognitive function. Stroke survivors experience greater acceleration in cognitive impairment compared with people without strokes and are at double the risk of developing dementia.

Cerebrovascular System

While the term "cardiovascular system" is likely familiar, "cerebrovascular system" may be less so. The cerebrovascular system refers to blood vessels that carry blood to and from the brain. Just as maintaining healthy blood vessels is essential for heart health, it is also a key component in preserving brain health.

Researchers found that the presence of vascular disease—including high blood pressure, high LDL cholesterol, high triglyceride levels, and coronary artery disease—is the most prominent risk factor in the transition from mild cognitive impairment (MCI) to dementia.

Vascular Dementia

The brains of people with vascular dementia often show evidence of prior strokes, thickening blood vessel walls, and thinning white matter.

Not everyone who suffers a stroke will develop vascular dementia. A person's risk for dementia after stroke depends on the size and number of strokes that person experiences and the brain regions affected. Vascular dementia also can result from other conditions that impede blood flow and the delivery of oxygen to the brain.

High blood pressure, problems with the heartbeat's rhythm, diabetes, and high cholesterol can increase a person's risk of vascular dementia. By controlling or managing risk factors, you may lower your chance of developing cognitive impairment and dementia.

Small-Vessel Disease

Strokes are often catastrophic, whereas small-vessel disease is more insidious.

High blood pressure is one of the biggest risk factors for small-vessel leakage, although diabetes can also weaken blood vessel walls, increasing the risk for leaks. Leakage is not typically responsible for memory problems, however; it is more likely to impact executive function—the ability to organize, plan, and multitask.

Blood vessel changes also can increase the degree of impairment or the speed of cognitive decline in other forms of dementia, such as Alzheimer's disease.

Hypertension and the Brain

You probably know that hypertension—high blood pressure—is an important risk factor for cardiovascular disease. Hypertension is also the leading cause of stroke and the single most important risk factor for stroke, making it a threat to your brain as well (see "Control Blood Pressure Now for Brain Benefits").

High blood pressure in midlife is also associated with a greater risk of

---

Stroke Prevention

According to the American Stroke Association, every 40 seconds someone in the United States has a stroke. To reduce your risk, the association advises:

- **Get enough sleep.** Adults need 7 to 9 hours per night.
- **Schedule regular visits with your health-care provider.** Talk about how to control or manage your risk factors.
- **Move more, sit less.** Aim for 150 minutes of moderate aerobic exercise or 75 minutes of vigorous exercise (or a combination) per week.
- **Eat healthy.** Increase the amount of fruits and vegetables you eat. Reduce your intake of sodium, added sugar, and saturated fats.
- **Don't smoke or vape.** If you currently smoke or vape, quit.

Vascular Dementia Warning Signs

The second most common type of dementia diagnosis is vascular dementia. According to Alzheimers.gov, signs of vascular dementia include:

- **Difficulty performing tasks** that used to be easy, such as paying bills
- **Trouble following instructions** or learning new information and routines
- **Problems with language,** such as finding the right word or using the wrong word
- **Changes in personality,** behavior, and mood, such as depression, agitation, and anger

Your doctor's office will take your blood pressure at almost every visit, and you should always ask what the numbers are and what they mean.

NEW FINDING

Control Blood Pressure Now for Brain Benefits

It's never too soon to start eating right for better blood pressure—and a healthier brain. Women with diets designed to lower blood pressure during middle age were less likely to report memory loss and other signs of cognitive decline decades later, researchers report. Investigators analyzed dietary data from about 5,000 women enrolled in the long-running NYU Women's Health Study, initially average age 49. Participants were followed for more than 30 years and then asked to report any cognitive complaints, which were assessed using standard questions indicative of later mild cognitive impairment. Women who initially ate a heart-healthy diet adhering most closely to the DASH regimen were 17 percent less likely to report multiple cognitive issues.

Alzheimer's & Dementia, Oct. 20, 2023

dementia, which may be due to mini-strokes, strokes, damage to the blood vessels, or too little blood and oxygen being delivered to the brain. Even high variability in blood pressure is associated with greater dementia risk. Research also has shown that high blood pressure is associated with greater damage to the brain's white matter.

For the first time, researchers have identified specific regions of the brain that are damaged by high blood pressure and may contribute to a decline in mental processes and the development of dementia. A study published in the *European Heart Journal* in March 2023 gathered information from a combination of magnetic resonance imaging (MRI) scans of brains, genetic analyses, and observational data from thousands of patients. Researchers found changes to nine parts of the brain were related to higher blood pressure and worse cognitive function. These included the putamen, which is a round structure in the base of the front of the brain, responsible for regulating movement and influencing various types of learning. Other areas affected included regions of white matter that connect and enable signaling between different parts of the brain, and the anterior thalamic radiation, which is involved in executive functions. The researchers then checked their findings in a separate, large group of patients in Italy who had high blood pressure and found that the parts of the brain they had identified were indeed affected.

Another study, SPRINT (Systolic Blood Pressure Intervention Trial), which led some experts to lower recommendations for blood-pressure targets, also provided evidence that tight blood-pressure control in older adults helps reduce the risk of mild cognitive impairment (MCI). A sub-study, SPRINT Mind, reported that a systolic (top number) blood-pressure target of below 120 millimeters of mercury (mmHg) was associated with a 19 percent lower risk of developing MCI.

DASH vs. Hypertension

Among the brain-healthy dietary patterns we'll explore in this Special Health Report is a standout for its blood-pressure benefits: the Dietary Approaches to Stop Hypertension (DASH) plan, designed by the National Heart, Lung, and Blood Institute.

Results of the original DASH research showed that the greatest blood pressure reduction occurred with a DASH plan that was lowest in sodium—just 1,500 milligrams daily. Those initial findings were further bolstered by a comprehensive review of 30 randomized controlled trials totaling 5,545 participants. Compared with a control diet, the DASH diet reduced both systolic blood pressure and diastolic blood pressure (the bottom number) by 1.5 to 4.2 points.

The DASH diet is high in fruits, vegetables, and low-fat dairy. It emphasizes whole grains, fish, poultry, and nuts and limits red meats, added sugars and especially sodium. Overall, the DASH plan is rich in potassium, magnesium, calcium, and fiber.

DASH and Cognition

Even partly adhering to a DASH plan pays off for cognitive protection. People whose diets adhere to the DASH pattern have been found to score higher on the Modified Mini-Mental State Examination (MMMSE), a standard measure of cognitive abilities. DASH adherents' cognitive edge even increases over time.

Adding exercise to a DASH plan also seems to boost brain benefits more than either lifestyle change alone. One study of sedentary older adults with MCI but not dementia found that participants randomly assigned to aerobic exercise three times a week, plus the DASH diet, outperformed other groups.

Pounds and the Brain

Another modifiable risk factor for the heart-brain connection is excess weight.

14 | Special Report

Researchers have found that severely overweight people are less likely to be able to rewire their brains and find new neural pathways. Brain plasticity is impaired in obese people, making it less likely that they can learn new tasks or remember things.

Being obese can even affect the structure of your brain. MRI scans have shown clear associations between body fat percentage and brain form and structure, including gray and white matter.

Excess pounds at midlife or early old age also may increase the thinning of the brain's gray matter—effectively aging the brain by several years. Scientists have found that a higher body mass index (BMI) is significantly associated with gray-matter thinning. Similar but weaker links were seen for excess weight and total cerebral volume.

Cutting Calories

Not surprisingly then, losing excess weight—especially combined with additional exercise—has cognitive benefits. In one study, the combination of diet plus exercise was associated with the greatest improvement in cognitive scores. Exercise alone boosted scores similarly to exercise combined with dieting.

A related, if challenging, strategy against cognitive decline seems to be strictly cutting down on calories. One study found a connection between a restricted-calorie diet and improved memory among participants divided into three groups: One aimed to reduce calorie intake by 30 percent, mostly by eating smaller portions; a second group kept calories the same while increasing intake of healthy fats by 20 percent; and a third, the control group, made no dietary changes. At the end of three months, the calorie-cutting group scored an average of 20 percent better in tests of memory performance; the other groups showed no change. Researchers theorized that the calorie-cutters, who lost four to seven pounds, might experience brain benefits from decreased insulin and inflammation.

Diabetes and Dementia

Excess weight can also lead to diabetes, in which the body's ability to produce or respond to the hormone insulin is impaired, resulting in elevated levels of blood sugar (glucose). Since diabetes is a known contributor to heart disease, it's also bad for the brain.

One study linked higher blood-sugar levels with a 40 percent greater risk of developing dementia. Blood-glucose levels of people with diabetes who developed dementia over seven years averaged 190 milligrams per deciliter (mg/dL), compared with 160 mg/dL in those who did not develop dementia. People with high blood glucose levels—but short of diabetes—were still 20 percent more likely to develop dementia than those with normal blood-glucose levels.

Researchers have also compared results of MRI brain scans and cognitive tests conducted on people with diabetes with healthy subjects. Participants with diabetes had more white-matter abnormalities in the brain and more severe thinning of the cortex than the control group; they also scored worse on tests of memory and reaction times. Brain deterioration was worse among diabetic participants who were overweight.

Lowering Risk

Last year, however, a study in *Diabetes Care* showed that people with diabetes who keep lifestyle and other risk factors in check can reduce their dementia risk. Among the nearly 90,000 participants in the study, those with type 2 diabetes had an 88 percent greater risk of developing dementia than a control group. That increased risk vanished, however, for diabetes patients who had at least five of seven risk factors within recommended ranges: nonsmoking, elevated

---

DASH Basics

If you're interested in giving the DASH plan a try, these steps are designed to help you get started:

Eat More
- Fruits
- Vegetables
- Whole grains
- Nuts and legumes
- Low-fat dairy (2–3 daily servings)

Eat Less
- Red and processed meats
- Sweetened beverages
- Sodium

You can download the complete DASH plan for free at https://bit.ly/2DwM8pe.

NEW FINDING

Diabetes Management Lowers Dementia Risk

Managing diabetes might help reduce the higher risk of dementia associated with the disease. A Hong Kong study followed more than 55,000 patients with diabetes, average age 62, for more than eight years. Roughly half were assigned to a diabetes management program designed to improve glycemic control. During the follow-up period, 1,938 patients in the intervention group were diagnosed with some form of dementia, compared with 2,728 patients receiving usual care. Higher levels of HbA1C, a standard measure of blood-sugar control over time, were associated with a higher risk of dementia incidence. A moderate glycemic control target of HbA1C between 6.5 percent and 7.5 percent was associated with lower dementia incidence.

JAMA Network Open, Feb. 12, 2024

---

blood sugar, blood pressure, BMI, protein in the blood, physical activity, and diet.

Those with healthy lifestyles also saw fewer declines in cognitive processing speed, executive functioning, and brain volume. On the other hand, diabetes patients with two or fewer risk factors on target were at even higher dementia risk—142 percent—than the control group.

Maintaining a healthy weight and being physically active are the most effective ways to prevent diabetes (see "Diabetes Management Lowers Dementia Risk"). All these cardiovascular risk factors can be modified with a healthy dietary pattern and lifestyle changes.

Diet Makes a Difference

Does what you eat really matter to your heart and brain? A study published in January 2023 in *JAMA Internal Medicine* that followed almost 120,000 health professionals for up to 36 years found that a healthy diet was associated with lower risk of total and cause-specific mortality. Participants whose diets were scored in the top one-fifth of adherence to any of four healthy eating patterns recommended by the *Dietary Guidelines for Americans* had a 14 percent to 20 percent lower risk of total mortality compared-with those with the lowest adherence. Following a healthy diet was also associated with lower risk of death from cardiovascular disease, heart disease, cancer, and respiratory disease.

Beyond promoting overall longevity, dietary intake has a big impact on specific factors that influence vascular health. These include high blood pressure, high LDL cholesterol, high triglycerides, type 2 diabetes, and excess body fat. As we've seen, these vascular factors also play an important role in brain health.

Processed meats like deli meats, sausage, ham, hot dogs, and bacon are high in sodium—on average, 400 percent higher than unprocessed meats—and sodium intake increases blood pressure and stroke risk. Now a study published in May 2023 in *Clinical Nutrition* suggests other ways processed meats might affect blood pressure.

Among 1,774 adults who consumed processed meat, researchers compared their estimated dietary nitrite and nitrate intake from processed meat to their blood pressure. Participants were divided into three groups of dietary nitrite intake (essentially high, medium, and low) and by level of total sodium intake (less than 1,500 grams daily; 1,500 to 2,300; greater than or equal to 2,300 grams a day). Diastolic blood pressure (the second number in a blood pressure reading) was elevated with higher sodium intake—and with higher dietary nitrite intake. There were no significant associations with systolic blood pressure (the first number).

It's sodium, of course, that's most associated with high blood pressure. When there's too much sodium in the blood, the body dilutes it by drawing water into the blood vessels. This increases the volume of blood, which puts extra pressure on the blood vessel walls. While high blood pressure generally has no symptoms, it increases the risk for heart attack, stroke, heart failure, kidney damage, vision loss, and sexual dysfunction.

One study published in *The New England Journal of Medicine*, Jan. 20, 2022, found that each daily increment of 1,000 milligrams (mg) of sodium excretion in the urine was associated with an 18 percent increase in risk for cardiovascular events like heart attack and stroke. On the other hand, each daily increment of 1,000 mg in potassium excretion was associated with an 18 percent decrease in risk. Consuming more sodium and less potassium was associated with a higher risk of cardiovascular events.

We get most of our sodium from salt, though not primarily from the saltshaker in your kitchen or dining room. Processed foods and restaurant meals are the major sources of dietary sodium.

Fortunately, research shows even modest reductions in salt intake can result in reduced blood pressure over time. To cut your salt intake:

- **Eat fewer prepared foods.** Ready-to-eat or restaurant snacks, meals, sauces, and dressings are often high in sodium. Choose low-sodium varieties and smaller portions. Opt for good snacks containing healthy ingredients.
- **Find the facts.** Read the Nutrition Facts labels on packaged foods and menus to help make better choices.
- **Embrace home cooking.** Cooking at home means you have more control over your salt intake. Spices, aromatics, vinegars, and oils are a few flavorful ways to cut salt intake.
- **Eat more whole foods.** Cut sodium intake while eating more foods rich in potassium, like fruits, vegetables, whole grains, beans, and leafy greens.
- **Get adequate calcium.** Calcium is involved in regulating blood pressure by affecting the flexibility of vascular cells. Calcium is most common in dairy products and calcium-fortified milk substitutes, leafy greens, and almonds.
- **Consider salt substitutes.** Research has shown that people using a salt substitute (75 percent sodium chloride and 25 percent potassium chloride) have a lower rate of stroke and other major cardiovascular events.

Controlling Cholesterol

To control blood LDL ("bad") cholesterol levels, the major focus should be on reducing intake of saturated fats like those in fatty cuts of meats, processed meats, butter, lard, and coconut and palm oils. Replace saturated fats with poly- and monounsaturated fats like those found in liquid vegetable oils.

You can also replace saturated fats with unsaturated fats by incorporating fatty fish—like salmon, tuna, and mackerel—in place of red and processed meats. Avocados and a variety of nuts and seeds are also good sources of unsaturated fats.

Substituting unsaturated fats for saturated fats can help protect the brain as well as the heart: A 2021 study published online by the Cambridge University Press found participants who consumed more saturated fat performed worse on tests of verbal memory and had lower gray-matter volumes in the left prefrontal cortex, an area that supports memory processes, compared with participants whose diets were high in omega-3 polyunsaturated fats.

While health-care providers used to recommend all individuals reduce intake of cholesterol-rich foods such as eggs to avoid high blood cholesterol levels, that recommendation has changed. While some individuals are particularly sensitive to dietary cholesterol, current research suggests the amount of dietary cholesterol consumed by the typical U.S. adult has little effect on LDL cholesterol levels in the blood.

Dietary fiber can slow cholesterol absorption. Fiber also interferes with the absorption of bile acids, which are compounds that help us digest fat. The liver must then use cholesterol to make new bile acids, thereby lowering your blood cholesterol levels. Choose whole grains and whole-grain products over refined, and eat plenty of fruits, vegetables, and legumes (beans and lentils) in place of other carbohydrate foods.

"Good" HDL cholesterol returns LDL cholesterol from the artery walls back to the liver to be removed from the body. Raising HDL cholesterol levels through a healthier lifestyle may reduce cardiovascular disease (CVD) risk. Increasing

Identifying Sugars

In addition to checking Nutrition Facts labels, which now break out added sugars, compare the total amount of sugars in similar products. Check ingredients lists for terms indicating sugar of any type, such as glucose, fructose, evaporated cane juice, malt syrup, honey, and agave.

NEW FINDING

Cholesterol Role in Dementia Complicated

When it comes to HDL cholesterol—commonly called the "good" cholesterol—there seems to be a "Goldilocks" effect with dementia risk. Researchers examined data from over 184,000 individuals ages 55 and older, focusing on those without a dementia history. The study tracked them for dementia development, analyzing cholesterol levels, particularly HDL and LDL, and considering factors like age and statin use. While previous research hinted at a link between these cholesterol types and dementia risk, the specifics were unclear, especially regarding how statin use might affect this relationship. The findings revealed that both low and high levels of HDL cholesterol were associated with increased dementia risk. However, the relationship with LDL cholesterol was less straightforward: LDL cholesterol didn't show a significant overall association with dementia risk, but statin users with higher LDL cholesterol had a slightly higher risk of Alzheimer's disease-related dementia.

Neurology, Oct. 19, 2023

NEW FINDING

Dietary Choices Cut Cognitive Risk

Consuming an anti-inflammatory diet or a protein-rich diet may be linked to lower risk of cognitive impairment. That's the takeaway from a Chinese study of nearly 8,700 participants in a health survey, average age 83.5. Anti-inflammatory diet scores were calculated based on intake of vegetables, fruits, legumes and their products, nuts, and tea at levels above "frequently or virtually every day." Protein foods included meats, fish, eggs, dairy and its products, and bean products. Participants with a higher anti-inflammatory diet score were at 21 percent reduced risk of cognitive impairment, while those with higher protein scores were at 9 percent lower risk. Moreover, as anti-inflammatory and protein scores rose, the risk of cognitive decline went down.

Nutrients, May 1, 2024

your intake of unsaturated fats from plant oils, nuts, seeds, beans, avocados, and olives may raise HDL levels.

Reducing Triglycerides

Healthy lifestyle choices can help lower triglyceride levels. We get triglycerides from fat in our diets, but refined carbohydrates can also increase triglyceride levels. Healthy, simple dietary swaps can be especially helpful for preventing and treating high triglyceride levels:

- **Be carb conscious.** Choose whole grains and foods made with them (such as oatmeal, quinoa, and whole-wheat pasta) instead of refined carbohydrates like white bread and white pasta.
- **Skip added sugars.** Choose naturally sweet foods, and look for foods with little or no added sugars when choosing packaged foods.
- **Choose healthy fats.** Opt for monounsaturated and polyunsaturated fats, which are found in plant oils, nuts, and fatty fish, like salmon and tuna.
- **Limit alcohol.** Swap out libations, which are high in ethanol and sugar (both of which are converted to triglycerides), with water, nonalcoholic seltzer, or unsweetened iced tea.

In addition to healthy lifestyle changes, your health-care provider may recommend medication, such as statins, fibrates, niacin, or prescription omega-3 fatty acids, to lower triglyceride levels (see "Cholesterol Role in Dementia Complicated").

Diet and Diabetes Risk

Diet and lifestyle go a long way in preventing type 2 diabetes, managing the disorder, or even reversing its onset.

Losing even modest amounts of weight can improve blood sugar and other diabetes outcomes in both type 1 and type 2 diabetes. Start by aiming to lose 5 percent of your current weight if you are overweight or have obesity.

Changing what you eat can dramatically improve blood sugar control and associated metabolic risk factors, even without weight loss. Diet patterns that are rich in minimally processed whole foods are associated with lower risk for type 2 diabetes. This means cutting back on refined grains and cereals, added sugars, salt, and processed meats, and eating plenty of healthy plant oils, fruits, nuts, seeds, vegetables, beans, minimally processed whole grains, seafood, and yogurt.

Avoiding frequent blood sugar spikes may help reduce the risk of developing diabetes. Soluble fiber—found in whole grains, as well as many fruits, vegetables, nuts, seeds, and beans—delays the absorption of carbohydrates, thereby reducing the blood-sugar spike after a meal. This may be one reason higher intake of whole grains has been consistently associated with a lower risk of diabetes in observational studies.

Managing Your Weight

To lose weight and keep it off, the secret isn't diet foods—it's finding behavior changes you can make permanent. Lifestyle changes like portion control, being more physically active, and swapping out foods with added sugars and refined grains for plant foods like beans, fruits, and vegetables are a healthy approach to weight loss (see "Dietary Choices Cut Cognitive Risk").

Choosing a dietary pattern that emphasizes fruits and vegetables is a big step toward cardiovascular and cognitive health.

3 Patterns That Protect

The American Heart Association's latest edition of "Dietary Guidance to Improve Cardiovascular Health" emphasizes the importance of dietary patterns over individual foods or nutrients; underscores the critical role of initiating heart-healthy dietary habits early in life; and discusses additional benefits of heart-healthy dietary patterns, beyond cardiovascular health. The latest *Dietary Guidelines for Americans* similarly emphasizes overall dietary patterns rather than eating more of this food and less of that, or consuming so-called "super foods." This approach is backed by a wealth of recent research.

Both the Mediterranean and MIND diets were associated with fewer signs of Alzheimer's disease in a postmortem study of 581 older adults, published March 8, 2023, in *Neurology*. Researchers used data from the Rush Memory and Aging Project, which followed participants who agreed to annual clinical and dietary evaluations and brain donation at death. Average ages were 84 at initial assessment and 91 at death. Adherence to both dietary patterns was significantly associated with less global Alzheimer's pathology and less accumulation of the beta-amyloid plaques linked to the disease. Both diets emphasize plant foods, and participants with the highest intake of leafy green vegetables—seven or more weekly servings—showed less global Alzheimer's pathology than those who ate one or two servings weekly.

Although individual foods and nutrients do offer cognitive benefits, eating for a healthy brain is not just a matter of consuming a few extra blueberries and switching to olive oil. It's your overall dietary pattern that makes a difference.

Mediterranean-Style Eating

There is no single version of the Mediterranean diet, given the cultural diversity of the 22 countries bordering this sea. The Mediterranean Diet Pyramid, proposed by the nonprofit Oldways

For some of us, it may take some adjustments. But, if you stick to a healthy diet, like the Mediterranean, you will not only "get used" to it but will crave those leafy greens and healthy proteins.

NEW FINDING

Diet, Lifestyle Add to Cognitive Reserve

A healthy lifestyle may provide older adults with a "cognitive reserve" to protect against dementia, according to a study of data from the long-running Rush Memory and Aging Project. The study followed 586 individuals for up to 24 years, including lifestyle factors, cognitive testing, and postmortem neuropathologic evaluations. A healthy lifestyle was defined as a high MIND diet score, noncurrent smoking, limited alcohol consumption, at least 150 minutes of weekly physical activity, and high late-life cognitive activity. Healthier lifestyle scores were associated with better late-life cognitive tests, fewer dementia-related brain pathologies, and lower levels of compounds associated with Alzheimer's disease.

JAMA Neurology, Feb. 5, 2024

---

group, is one easy-to-follow guide (see https://tinyurl.com/3ca8b7cj).

When researching the benefits of the dietary pattern traditionally found in areas around the Mediterranean compared with the typical American diet, scientists generally emphasize:

More
- Fruits
- Vegetables
- Legumes
- Monounsaturated fats (such as olive oil)
- Nuts and seeds
- Whole grains
- Fish

Fewer
- Red meats
- Saturated fats
- Sweets

Also
- Moderate alcohol consumption, especially of red wine with meals

Not all traditional dishes from this region are the healthiest choices, nor are all the Americanized versions. If you're trying to eat like a Mediterranean, skip the never-ending pasta bar and meat-laden pizza.

The chief difference between a Mediterranean-style diet and other healthy-eating plans, such as DASH, is the emphasis on unsaturated fats found in plant foods, especially monounsaturated fat in the form of olive oil.

Researching Mediterranean Benefits

The Mediterranean diet is among the most-researched dietary patterns. It regularly shows up at the top of rankings of popular diets. Here's a sampling of the research linking the diet to heart and brain benefits:

Slowing Cognitive Decline. In 2023, a study of 939 older Greeks found that closer adherence to a Mediterranean diet was associated with slower cognitive decline. Participants self-reported persistent cognitive decline not attributed to neurological, psychiatric, or medical disorders. Their diets were scored from 0 to 55 for adherence to a Mediterranean diet. After a little over three years of follow-up and adjustment for possible confounding factors, a 10-point higher Mediterranean diet score was associated with a 7 percent annual reduction in the progression of subjective cognitive decline (see "Diet, Lifestyle Add to Cognitive Reserve").

Similarly, researchers looked at data on about 5,000 Chicago Health and Aging Project participants who tried to follow a Mediterranean-style diet over 20 years; questionnaires every three years checked on consumption of 144 different foods. Participants with slower cognitive decline over the years were those who adhered most closely to the Mediterranean diet, while limiting foods that are part of Western (American) diets. The difference between those with the highest Mediterranean adherence and those who ate the most Western-style foods was the equivalent of almost six years of mental aging.

Another study used data from the Age-Related Eye Disease Studies (AREDS and AREDS2), designed to test the benefits of supplements against age-related macular degeneration (AMD) in the eyes. These well-designed studies also assessed the 8,000 total participants' diets and cognitive function, so researchers were able to examine the effects of nine components of the Mediterranean diet. Participants with the greatest overall adherence to the Mediterranean diet had the lowest risk of cognitive impairment. High fish and vegetable consumption appeared to have the greatest protective benefit; at 10 years, AREDS2 participants with the highest fish consumption had the slowest rate of cognitive decline.

Reducing Alzheimer's Risk. Other research has looked specifically at associations between the Mediterranean diet and lower risk of Alzheimer's disease. In a

20 | Special Report

three-year brain-imaging study, researchers looked for Alzheimer's disease-associated brain changes in 70 cognitively normal adults ages 30 to 60. Participants whose diets were closer to a Mediterranean style of eating showed fewer negative brain changes over the course of the study than those with lower adherence.

Another study reported that people who closely followed a Mediterranean-style diet had less amyloid and tau pathology (characteristic of Alzheimer's disease), increased brain volume in regions vulnerable to Alzheimer's disease, and better memory performance. Higher adherence was also linked to larger gray matter volume and better memory scores.

Mediterranean vs. Stroke Risk. Following a Mediterranean-style diet might also reduce the risk of stroke—crucial to brain health—especially for women. In a study from the United Kingdom of more than 23,000 adults, women over the age of 40 who most closely followed a Mediterranean diet were 22 percent less likely to suffer a stroke over 17 years of follow-up. Men who followed the diet were at 6 percent lower risk; overall, the Mediterranean diet was associated with a 17 percent risk reduction.

Weight Loss and Cardiovascular Benefits. A "green" Mediterranean diet that emphasizes plant-based proteins may be even more beneficial. Scientists who conducted a randomized clinical trial compared three diet groups: a control group given healthy dietary guidance, a group that followed a standard Mediterranean diet, and a group that followed a green version of the Mediterranean diet. Those in the green group were given three to four cups a day of green tea plus a plant-based protein shake. Both Mediterranean groups were given an ounce of walnuts (about 14 halves) per day.

After six months, both Mediterranean groups experienced similar weight loss, but the green group had a greater reduction in waist circumference, LDL ("bad") cholesterol, diastolic blood pressure, and insulin resistance, as well as a greater reduction in a 10-year cardiovascular risk score (see "Mediterranean Cardiovascular Risk Reduction").

Nordic Alternative

Like the Mediterranean diet, but with a Scandinavian twist, is the Nordic diet, developed by the University of Copenhagen in collaboration with the famed Noma restaurant. The diet is adapted to Scandinavian tastes and seasonal, sustainable foods. It emphasizes whole grains such as rye, barley, and oats; berries and other fruits; vegetables (especially cabbage and root vegetables like potatoes and carrots); fatty fish such as salmon, mackerel, and herring; and legumes (beans and peas). While less studied than other diets, the Nordic pattern may encourage weight loss and lower blood pressure—both of which benefit your brain.

Another twist on the pattern is the Atlantic diet (see "Introducing the Atlantic Diet," on the following page).

Med + DASH = MIND Diet

A combination of the Mediterranean diet and the DASH diet, aptly called the MIND (Mediterranean-DASH Intervention for Neurodegenerative Delay) diet, may prove especially potent in protecting brain power. Developed by scientists at Rush University, the MIND diet plan combines the best brain-health aspects of the Mediterranean and DASH diets with "the dietary components and servings linked to neuroprotection and dementia prevention."

The first tests of the MIND diet compared it to DASH and the Mediterranean diet. More than 900 participants, ages 58 to 98, were assessed for adherence to the three diets, then followed for an average of 4.5 years. During that span, 144 participants were diagnosed with Alzheimer's.

NEW FINDING

Mediterranean Cardiovascular Risk Reduction

Adhering to a Mediterranean-style diet may reduce cardiovascular risks, according to the first review of its kind to focus on the diet's benefits for females. Researchers pooled results from 16 prior randomized controlled trials and prospective cohort studies totaling more than 720,000 women initially free of cardiovascular disease (CVD). Greater adherence to a Mediterranean diet was associated with a 24 percent lower risk of developing CVD, as well as 23 percent lower total mortality. Coronary heart disease and stroke were also less common among women who most closely followed a Mediterranean dietary pattern. Researchers concluded: "This study supports a beneficial effect of the Mediterranean diet on primary prevention of CVD and death in women and is an important step in enabling sex-specific guidelines."

Heart, July 27, 2023

NEW FINDING

Introducing the Atlantic Diet

A variation on the Mediterranean diet moves the focus to the Atlantic, with similar benefits for cardiovascular health. Scientists investigated adherence to the traditional dietary pattern of northwestern Spain and Portugal, which they dubbed the "Atlantic diet." Like the Mediterranean diet, the Atlantic diet emphasizes the consumption of fresh, seasonal, and locally sourced foods such as fruits, vegetables, cereals, pulses (dry beans, lentils, and chickpeas), fish, dairy products, and olive oil. But the Atlantic diet typically includes a greater proportion of fish, milk, potatoes, fruits, and vegetables. Participants in the study of 574 adults who were randomized to follow the Atlantic diet for six months lowered their risk of developing metabolic syndrome, compared with those who stuck to their regular diets. Metabolic syndrome refers to a group of health risks including larger waist circumference, elevated triglyceride levels, low HDL cholesterol, high blood pressure, and high blood sugar.

JAMA Network Open, Feb. 7, 2024

The MIND diet was associated with a slower rate of cognitive decline, equivalent to 7.5 years of younger brain age. Those with the highest MIND diet scores were 53 percent less likely to develop Alzheimer's disease than those with the lowest scores.

The lower risk for those most closely following the MIND diet was with the highest adherence to a Mediterranean diet (54 percent) and the DASH plan (39 percent). But only the top one-third of Mediterranean and DASH scores were associated with lower Alzheimer's risk. The second-highest third of MIND scores were associated with lower risk (35 percent), however, suggesting that even modest dietary improvements following the MIND pattern could be beneficial.

Making Up MIND

Like the DASH and Mediterranean regimens, MIND emphasizes whole plant foods and limits the intake of animal and high-saturated-fat foods. It also places extra emphasis on consuming berries and green leafy vegetables, based on research linking these foods to cognitive protection. The MIND diet doesn't specify high fruit consumption other than berries, unlike other diets (see "Weight Loss Matches MIND").

MIND drops the DASH recommendation for high dairy consumption and calls for only weekly fish consumption, lower than recommended in the Mediterranean diet. Because the MIND diet specifies just two vegetable servings per day, two berry servings per week, and one fish meal per week—recommendations much lower than in the Mediterranean or DASH plans—researchers suggest it might be easier to stick with.

Key recommendations include:
- **Green leafy vegetables:** at least six servings per week
- **Other vegetables:** at least one serving per day
- **Berries:** at least two servings per week
- **Nuts:** at least five servings per week
- **Olive oil as the primary cooking oil**
- **Whole grains:** at least three servings per day
- **Fish (not fried):** at least once per week
- **Beans:** more than three meals per week
- **Chicken or turkey (not fried):** at least two meals per week
- **Wine:** one glass per day (optional)

In addition to these recommended intakes, the MIND plan specifies some dietary don'ts, identifying five unhealthy groups to limit:
- Red meats
- Butter and stick margarine
- Cheese
- Pastries and sweets
- Fried or fast food

It calls for eating less than 1 tablespoon of butter a day and less than one serving a week of cheese, fried food, or fast food.

Continuing Research

Scientists have continued to follow up the initial findings that helped establish the MIND diet. Researchers in Australia reported that greater adherence to the MIND diet was associated with a 19 percent lower risk of cognitive impairment, Alzheimer's disease, and other dementias. The study of 1,220 adults, ages 60 and older, followed participants for 12 years. No similar benefit was seen for sticking to a Mediterranean diet without the brain-health components of the MIND plan, such as eating berries.

Following the MIND diet may specifically benefit stroke survivors, who are twice as likely to develop dementia as the general population. Among 106 stroke survivors followed for an average of six years, participants who scored highest for MIND diet adherence had substantially slower rates of cognitive decline than those who scored lowest. This association remained strong even after considering participants' level of education and participation in cognitive and physical activities. Similar benefits were not associated with adherence to either the Mediterranean or DASH diets, however.

NU-AGE for Brain Health

Another twist on the principles of the Mediterranean diet, the Nutrition in Elderly People (NU-AGE) diet, was created for a European study of about 1,200 older adults. Half of the group was assigned to eat their regular diet; the other half was assigned to the NU-AGE diet.

The NU-AGE diet focuses on nutrients important for aging, such as vitamins D and B$_{12}$, calcium, and fiber. Researchers fit them into a diet that's similar to a Mediterranean diet, with specific examples tailored to each person. For instance, instead of just recommending more polyunsaturated fats, the diet says fatty fish should be consumed twice weekly.

After one year, people in the NU-AGE group showed significant improvements in cognition and memory, compared with people who didn't follow the diet.

NU-AGE Specifics

The NU-AGE diet calls for limiting intakes of meat, poultry, alcohol, salt, and sweets, and recommends:

Daily minimums
- Fruit: 8.5 oz
- Vegetables: 10.6 oz
- Low-fat dairy: 16.9 oz
- Low-fat cheese: 1 oz
- Olive oil: 0.7 oz

Weekly minimums
- Two servings of fish (4.4 oz per serving)
- Two servings of nuts (0.7 oz per serving)
- Two to four eggs

The NU-AGE diet can be more restrictive than other diets. Recommendations include a maximum of four servings of low-fat meat or poultry per week, with pasta no more than twice a week.

Some people may find these guidelines hard to follow. NU-AGE may not be right for people with kidney disease or diabetes, as these patients may need specific amounts of fruits, vegetables, and grains.

Nutrient-Dense Patterns

As you consider healthy dietary patterns, keep in mind the principle of "nutrient density," which is especially important as you get older. After age 50, most adults' calorie needs decrease: Men generally need 2,400 to 2,800 daily calories and women 1,800 to 2,000, depending on physical activity levels.

Even as calorie needs decline, however, your vitamin and mineral requirements stay the same or may even increase—which can make it a challenge to get the nutrients you need. That's why it's important to choose foods that are nutrient dense: They deliver plenty of good nutrition for their calorie counts.

Nutrient-dense foods include fruits, vegetables, whole grains, beans, nuts, seafood, lean poultry and meat, dairy products, and eggs. In general, nutrient-dense choices are more likely to be whole foods than highly processed foods.

Picking Your Pattern

Whatever dietary pattern best suits your needs and preferences, following the basic principles these healthy patterns have in common can help protect your heart health and brain power (not all popular diets embody all these healthy principles).

A healthy dietary pattern involves a series of smart choices about what are called "macronutrients"—protein, carbohydrates, and fats. In the next chapter, we'll look at how each of these may affect your heart health and brain power.

NEW FINDING

Weight Loss Matches MIND

Cutting calories might be as effective for cognitive protection as adopting the MIND diet. A study randomly assigned 600 cognitively healthy, overweight or obese older adults with "suboptimal" diets and a family history of dementia to follow either the MIND diet or their regular diet, both with mild caloric restriction, for three years. The MIND diet group was given blueberries, nuts, and olive oil. Both groups received individualized dietary counseling. The control group focused on calorie tracking, portion control, and behavioral strategies for weight loss. The groups lost similar amounts of weight. Improvements in cognition were not statistically significant between the two groups, and brain MRIs showed similar brain changes. When looking at these results, it's important to consider that the control-diet group may have improved their dietary intake as they focused on losing weight, and the weight-loss itself may have positively impacted brain health in both groups.

New England Journal of Medicine, Aug. 17, 2023

CARBS   PROTEIN   FATS

Understanding the perks and worries surrounding your choices of macronutrients form the basis of a healthy dietary pattern.

© VectorMine | Dreamstime

4 Macronutrients for Heart and Brain

You can hardly turn on the TV or click on Facebook these days without seeing competing claims about fats, carbohydrates ("carbs"), or protein. Self-proclaimed diet experts and food marketers will try to convince you that you need fewer carbohydrates, different types of fat, more protein, or other fads. The fact is that these three "macronutrients" are the nutrients your body and brain need in the largest amounts to function properly, and they provide your body with energy in the form of calories from food. (Micronutrients, such as vitamins and minerals, are needed in smaller amounts, and are not assigned calorie values.)

The relative proportions of these macronutrients are used to calculate how many calories are in a food. Rather than measure calories by literally burning up a food, most food manufacturers simply do the math: Fats have 9 calories per gram, while carbohydrates and proteins contain 4 calories per gram. Fiber, a form of carbohydrate, largely passes through the body without being digested, so its calories don't count.

Most of the fad diets of recent years have focused on these fundamental nutrients, advocating eating more or less of these foods, depending on the fad. These include the low-fat, low-carb, high-protein and high-fat, high-protein diets.

Understanding Carbs

Among macronutrients, carbohydrates have lately replaced fats as the nutritional villain du jour. It's popular to go low-carb or adopt some other diet that emphasizes other macronutrients at the expense of carbohydrate intake. Beyond the popular Atkins diet, recent carb-cutting regimens include the ketogenic, or "keto," diet and the Whole30 diet.

Some of these diets may have weight-loss benefits, and cutting back on refined carbohydrates, starches, and sugars can improve overall health. But before you start tossing out all carbs, keep in mind that carbohydrates provide energy for the body, especially the brain and the nervous system. To obtain that energy, enzymes break down carbohydrates into glucose (sugar) during digestion, which the body then uses to fuel its many functions.

Simple Carbs

Simple carbohydrates are made up of one (single) or two (double) sugar molecules. They include:

- **Sucrose,** a double sugar—the sugar you sprinkle on cereal or spoon into your coffee
- **Glucose,** a single sugar found in most fruits
- **Fructose,** a single sugar also found in fruits
- **Galactose,** a single sugar found in dairy products
- **Lactose,** a double sugar found in dairy products
- **Maltose,** a double sugar found in vegetables and in beer

---

24 | Special Report

Your Brain on Carbs

Glucose is the brain's primary energy source; it's among the few substances able to pass unhindered through the blood-brain barrier that protects the brain. Because brain cells can't store glucose like other cells can, however, the brain requires a steady stream throughout the day.

Areas of the brain that control thinking are sensitive to drops in glucose, which is why you might have trouble concentrating or thinking clearly if it's been several hours since your last meal. Tufts researchers have found that very-low-carbohydrate diets could have a negative impact on thinking and cognition. After only a day or two, even the glucose stored by the body is exhausted and must be replenished from the diet.

The brain's glucose needs are the basis for the Recommended Dietary Allowance (RDA) for carbohydrates. For adults, the RDA is 130 grams (g) daily (the equivalent of 520 calories). The Institute of Medicine (IOM) suggests that carbohydrates account for 45 to 65 percent of your total calories—a much higher share than advocated by low-carb diets.

Simple or Complex

You may have heard that some carbs are "simple" while others are "complex." Simple carbohydrates are made up of one (single) or two (double) sugar molecules. The most familiar simple carbohydrate is sucrose (a double sugar), the sugar you sprinkle on cereal or spoon into your coffee.

The nutritional value of simple carbohydrates depends on the foods in which they are found, so simple carbohydrates are not necessarily bad for you or to be avoided. Simple sugars such as those found in candy, non-diet sodas, syrups, and table sugar provide calories but few nutrients. In contrast, nutritious foods, such as fruits, vegetables, milk, and other dairy products, provide not only calories from sugar, but also essential vitamins and minerals.

Complex carbohydrates are made up of sugar molecules that are strung together in long chains. Complex carbohydrates are found in foods such as peas, beans, whole grains, and vegetables.

One neuroimaging study found that minimizing the consumption of simple carbohydrates might prevent or even reverse the brain changes associated with aging. Scientists theorized that, as people get older, their brains start to lose the ability to metabolize glucose efficiently, causing neurons to slowly starve and brain networks to destabilize.

Balancing Macronutrients

Other studies have reported that consuming too many carbohydrates relative to protein and fat seems to contribute to cognitive decline. Last year we saw a study of almost 3,000 participants in the China Health and Nutrition Survey, initially ages 55 to 93, that looked at breakfast and cognition over about nine years. More than three-quarters of calories consumed came from carbohydrates. Those who consumed 5 percent more calories from protein or fat at the expense of carbohydrate calories saw positive changes in their cognitive scores.

Don't Forget Fiber

One downside of cutting down on carbohydrates, however, is that it too often also means consuming less fiber, which is found only in carb-containing plant foods. Dietary fiber is not only good for your digestion, but a diet high in fiber also plays a major role in regulating blood glucose levels, which contributes to a reduced risk of diabetes and heart disease. Research also has shown that consuming soluble fiber (the type that absorbs water) modestly reduces levels of LDL ("bad") cholesterol in your blood.

Eating more fiber can make you feel full more quickly and help the feeling of

---

Carbohydrates: Quality Counts

High-Quality, Complex Carbohydrate Sources

- **All fruits,** including apples, bananas, berries, cherries, grapes, grapefruit, kiwifruit, mango, melon, oranges, peaches, pineapple, plums
- **All vegetables,** including artichokes, asparagus, broccoli, Brussels sprouts, cabbage, carrots, collard and turnip greens, cucumber, kale, lettuce, mushrooms, snap beans, spinach, tomatoes, yellow squash, zucchini
- **All whole grains:** including barley, bulgur wheat, farro, millet, oats, quinoa, whole wheat, and products made from these grains
- **Legumes,** including all beans, peas, and lentils
- **Dairy** milk and milk products, including cheese and yogurts that contain no added sugars

Low-Quality, Simple Carbohydrate Sources

- **Sugar-sweetened beverages,** including regular soft drinks, fruit "drinks" and "punches," energy drinks, sports drinks, lemonade, and sweetened coffees and teas (hot or cold)
- **Baked goods made with refined white flour,** such as white bread, bagels, crackers, cookies, cakes, and pastries
- **Processed potato products,** including french fries, tater tots, and instant potatoes
- **Ready-to-eat cereals,** granola and breakfast bars, and energy bars made with white flour and/or added sugars
- **Sugar,** including table sugar, honey, syrups, and nectars

Finding Fiber

Foods high in fiber may help protect your brain as well as your digestive system. Some fiber-rich choices include:

FOOD	AMOUNT	FIBER
Ready-to-eat cereal, high fiber, unsweetened	½ cup	14 g
Navy beans, cooked	½ cup	9.6 g
Raspberries	1 cup	8 g
Lentils, cooked	½ cup	7.8 g
Pinto beans, cooked	½ cup	7.7 g
Popcorn	3 cups	5.8 g
Peas	1 cup	8.8 g
Ready-to-eat cereal, bran flakes	¾ cup	5.5 g
Broccoli, cooked	1 cup	5.2 g
Carrots, cooked	1 cup	4.8 g
Apple, with skin	1 medium	4.8 g

Source: dietaryguidelines.gov

NEW FINDING

The Brain Benefits of Whole Grains

A new study of 3,326 participants from the Chicago Health and Aging Project reports that whole grains might help protect the brain. Participants, average age 75, completed a dietary questionnaire and underwent at least two cognitive assessments over an average of six years. Those who reported consuming three or more daily servings of whole grains had a slower rate of decline in global cognition, perceptual speed, and episodic memory compared with those who ate fewer than one serving per day. These results were statistically significant for the group as a whole and for Black participants (who made up 60 percent of the study population). The results did not quite reach statistical significance among white participants, who made up a smaller share of the study group.

Neurology, Nov. 28, 2023

---

fullness ("satiety") last longer. As a result, you may eat fewer total calories, which reduces your risk of obesity and heart disease.

Consuming fiber might also benefit your brain, according to a 2022 study in *Nutritional Neuroscience*. Researchers followed 3,739 Japanese adults, initially ages 40 to 64, for almost 20 years and found that higher fiber intake was associated with lower risk of disabling dementia. During the follow-up period, 670 cases of disabling dementia were diagnosed. Compared with the lowest one-quarter of dietary fiber intake, those consuming the most were 26 percent less likely to develop disabling dementia. Even the middle groups of fiber consumption were at somewhat lower risk (19 percent and 17 percent).

Soluble fiber was most strongly associated with lower risk. Those consuming the most total fiber averaged 21.4 grams a day—less than the U.S. recommended levels of 28 grams and 22 grams for men and women, respectively, over the age of age 50—while the lowest group averaged only 8.9 grams daily.

An earlier study similarly found that participants with the highest intake of dietary fiber had an almost 80 percent greater likelihood of "successful aging." That was defined as reaching old age free of chronic disease, disability, cognitive impairment, symptoms of depression, and respiratory symptoms.

Starch vs. Whole Grains

In addition to avoiding added sugars, recent research focused on another type of carbohydrate—starch—not specifically listed on Nutrition Facts panels. Those labels list total carbohydrates, total sugars, and dietary fiber. Subtract sugars and fiber from the total carbs and what remains is the starch content. Risks from excess consumption of starch—particularly refined starch, as in processed foods—include type 2 diabetes and weight gain, both factors in cardiovascular disease that can affect the brain (see "The Brain Benefits of Whole Grains").

Choosing whole grains and foods higher in fiber relative to starch can help modify your starch intake. A simple rule of thumb is to look for foods with a ratio of total carbohydrates to fiber of 10:1 or less. So, for example, a product such as white bread with 15 grams of carbohydrates and 1 gram of fiber would have a ratio of 15:1—not a good choice. Choose instead a whole-grain bread, which might have 12 grams of carbohydrates and 2 grams of fiber, a ratio of 6:1.

Consumption of whole grains, as well as nuts and legumes, has even been linked to possible brain benefits. An 11-year assessment of diet and cognitive function among nearly 4,000 older men and women found that these healthy choices were positively associated with higher cognitive functions. The researchers concluded these carbohydrate sources may be core neuroprotective foods common to various healthy plant-centered diets around the globe.

The bottom line on carbs and heart-brain health is to choose your sources of carbohydrates carefully to get the most nutritional benefits while not overloading on sugar and starch. That means emphasizing fruits and vegetables, whole grains, beans and other legumes, and limiting refined grains, added sugars, and starchy foods.

Fresh Thinking on Fats

Did you know that not all fats affect the body—or the brain—in the same way? You probably remember the low-fat diet craze, which demonized all fats and led to an array of packaged foods marketed as "healthy" because of their reduced fat content. Those low-fat products, such as low-fat cookies, typically substituted processed carbs and sugar for fat. Instead of improving health, the low-fat fad contributed to the expansion of the obesity epidemic.

Scientists now emphasize that it's more important to choose the right fats than it is to limit total fat intake. Some types of fat—monounsaturated and polyunsaturated fats, like those found in liquid vegetable oils, nuts, fish, and avocados—are good for your heart. That probably means they are also good for your brain. Fat is an important component of cell membranes in the brain and of the myelin coating on neurons, which speeds up the transmission of information in the nervous system.

Unsaturated Fats and Cognition

Recent research bolsters the case for cognitive protection from healthy unsaturated fats. Last year, for example, in a study in *Experimental Gerontology*, we saw more evidence that olive oil can help protect the brain. In the clinical trial with 84 participants, researchers compared evidence of Alzheimer's disease as well as mild cognitive impairment (MCI) between a group administered extra-virgin olive oil and a control group. Levels of markers of MCI and Alzheimer's improved in the olive-oil group (see "Olive Oil Proves Protective").

In annual testing, hallmarks of Alzheimer's disease in those receiving olive oil were restored to levels equal to those of a cognitively healthy group. Those not administered olive oil, however, saw increases in these hallmarks of Alzheimer's. Similarly, a marker of oxidative stress declined in the olive-oil group while increasing in patients not consuming olive oil.

Mediterranean Diet Fats

The heart-healthy Mediterranean diet, which we looked at in the previous chapter, also provides evidence of brain benefits from unsaturated fats. Participants in the large PREDIMED-NAVARRA trial who followed a Mediterranean diet and consumed at least four tablespoons of extra-virgin olive oil a day scored significantly better on two tests of mental abilities than a control group assigned to a low-fat diet. Those assigned to a Mediterranean diet supplemented with about a quarter-cup daily of walnuts, almonds, and hazelnuts—nuts rich in polyunsaturated fats—also scored better than the control group. After more than 6½ years of follow-up, fewer participants consuming either of the Mediterranean-style diets were diagnosed with dementia than individuals in the control group.

Fish Oil Omega-3s

A special type of unsaturated fats called omega-3 fatty acids are essential fats, so called because the body can't make them; you must obtain them from your diet. The two most common omega-3s found in fish, eicosapentaenoic acid (EPA) and docosahexaenoic acid (DHA), have been studied for possible brain benefits. (Another omega-3 fatty acid, alpha-linolenic acid, ALA, is found in plants such as walnuts, flaxseed, and many common vegetable oils; the body can convert ALA to the more complex DHA and EPA, though this process is inefficient.)

One reason scientists suspect the omega-3 DHA might be important for cognition is that it's the most plentiful fatty acid in the brain. DHA is especially prevalent in neurons and gray matter—the area responsible for language, memory, and thought. DHA is essential for the proper growth and function of brain tissue, including the production of neurons and the transmission of nerve impulses across neurons. High blood levels of DHA have been linked to a reduced risk of dementia and Alzheimer's disease.

In a study published Oct. 5, 2022, in *Neurology*, higher omega-3 concentrations in red blood cells were positively linked with brain structure and cognitive function—specifically, larger hippocampal

Not only is fish a better choice than fish oil supplements for nutrition, but it's a lot more tasty than a bunch of pills.

NEW FINDING

Olive Oil Proves Protective

A study of more than 92,000 health professionals reports that olive-oil consumption was associated with reduced risk of death from dementia. Consuming more than 7 grams (about half a tablespoon) per day of olive oil was associated with a 28 percent lower risk of dementia-related death compared with never or rarely consuming olive oil. Participants were initially free of cardiovascular disease and cancer; diet was assessed every four years, while death records were used to determine causes. Researchers further calculated that replacing 5 grams daily of margarine and mayonnaise with an equivalent amount of olive oil was associated with an 8 percent to 14 percent lower risk of dementia mortality. Substitutions for other vegetable oils or butter were not significant. The relationship between olive oil and dementia mortality risk was independent of overall diet quality, scientists noted; this may suggest that olive oil has properties that are uniquely beneficial for brain health. Some antioxidant compounds in olive oil can cross the blood-brain barrier, potentially having a direct effect on the brain, the scientists added.

JAMA Network Open, May 6, 2024

Fats in Oils

FAT	UNSATURATED MONO-	UNSATURATED POLY-	SAT FAT
Canola oil	62%	32%	6%
Safflower oil	13%	77%	10%
Sunflower oil	20%	69%	11%
Corn oil	25%	62%	13%
Olive oil	77%	9%	14%
Soybean oil	24%	61%	15%
Peanut oil	49%	33%	18%
Lard	47%	12%	41%
Palm oil	39%	10%	51%
Butter	28%	4%	68%
Coconut oil	6%	2%	92%

volume and better abstract reasoning. The cross-sectional study looked at about 2,200 people with an average age of 46. Even those with the APOE4 gene associated with greater Alzheimer's risk appeared to benefit from higher omega-3 levels, based on markers in the brain's white matter.

A review of 21 observational studies found that eating one additional serving per week of fish was associated with a 7 percent lower risk of Alzheimer's disease and a 5 percent overall lower risk of dementia over about 20 years. Each daily increment of 8 grams of polyunsaturated fats was associated with a 29 percent lower risk of mild cognitive impairment.

Total polyunsaturated fat intake (including omega-3s) also has been inversely linked to the risk of mild cognitive impairment.

Limit Saturated Fats

Experts in cardiovascular disease recommend substituting unsaturated fats for saturated fats as much as possible. Cook with liquid vegetable oils instead of butter, for example, and serve more fish and less fatty red meat.

One review of the evidence found that greater saturated-fat intake was associated with greater risk of Alzheimer's disease in three of four studies. The review also found an association between saturated-fat intake and the risks of developing dementia, cognitive decline, and mild cognitive impairment.

Similarly, findings from the Women's Health Study showed that women who consumed the most saturated fat had poorer scores on cognitive tests than those who consumed the least. Women consuming more saturated fat were about 65 percent more likely to experience a decline in mental performance over time. The total fat intake did not matter, but the type of fat did.

The American Heart Association recommends limiting saturated-fat intake to 5 percent to 6 percent of your total calories. In a 2,000-calorie daily diet, that would equal 100 to 120 calories a day from saturated fat (roughly 11 to 13 grams of saturated fat). That's a little less than the saturated fat in five teaspoons of butter, two cheeseburgers, or two slices of pepperoni pizza.

Fats and Blood Cholesterol

A key reason to avoid saturated fat is that it is believed to be the major dietary contributor to unhealthy blood (serum) cholesterol levels, although this link is often debated. While science continues to explore this connection, at present, the best advice is to substitute unsaturated fats for saturated fats.

Serum cholesterol in the blood is not the same as the dietary cholesterol listed on Nutrition Facts panels. As we've seen, recent expert guidance downgraded concerns over moderate intake of dietary cholesterol, such as that found in eggs and shellfish. That, too, remains a subject of scientific scrutiny, however, so don't overdo it.

Cholesterol and Cognition. As excess serum cholesterol accumulates, it begins to form plaque, which narrows blood vessels and makes them less flexible. This results in atherosclerosis, popularly known as "hardening of the arteries." Since your brain uses such a high proportion of your body's blood flow, anything that affects your circulation also impacts your brain.

The Diabetes Heart Study MIND research found that such changes were related to cognition even before becoming clinically apparent. Researchers measured the amount of calcified plaque in participants' coronary arteries when the study began. Seven years later, a battery of cognitive tests measured subjects' memory, processing speed, and executive function. Those who had more plaque at baseline, when the study began, scored lower on those mental tests.

Protein Fads and Facts

If carbs are the macronutrient villain du jour, protein is the hero. The Paleo and keto diets, as well as a plethora of packaged goods, tout the benefits of protein consumption. Most Americans, however, probably already get plenty of protein. The Daily Value (DV) for protein is 50 grams. Most of us far exceed that number, with actual consumption estimated at 62 to 66 grams of protein per day for women and 88 to 92 grams for men.

The downside of the current protein fixation is that we also consume too many calories and the saturated fats that accompany animal sources of protein. A quarter pound of 70 percent lean ground beef, for example, delivers more than 16 grams of protein—nearly one-fourth the DV. But that serving also contains about 375 calories and almost 13 grams of saturated fat.

Higher consumption of processed red meat was associated with a 20 percent higher risk of dying from dementia. Poultry consumption, however, was linked to a 15 percent lower risk. Higher consumption of eggs was associated with a lower risk of death from dementia.

Other research has added to cognitive concerns about eating too much processed meat. One study looked at data on almost a half-million participants in the UK Biobank study, comparing meat intake with incidence of Alzheimer's and other dementias. Over about eight years, each additional 25 grams (a little less than one ounce) of processed meat consumption per day was associated with a 44 percent greater risk of developing dementia. The association held regardless of genetic predisposition to Alzheimer's.

Prefer Plant Protein

Compared with protein from meat, a healthier option is to obtain more of your protein from plant sources. One study reported that postmenopausal women who ate high levels of plant protein had lower risks of dementia-related death. Compared with women who had the least amount of plant protein intake in their diet, those with the highest amount had a 21 percent lower risk of dementia-related death.

Among the many healthy sources of plant protein are beans and other legumes, soy products, whole grains, and nuts. Even a vegetable such as broccoli, not noted for its protein content, contains nearly 3 grams per cup.

You need to consume high-quality protein and ensure your diet contains all the essential amino acids your body requires from dietary sources. "Complete" proteins with all these amino acids are found in meat, poultry, fish, eggs, dairy products, and soy.

Grains, with a few exceptions such as quinoa, buckwheat, and amaranth, are not an adequate source of the amino acids lysine and isoleucine. Legumes, such as beans, tend to fall short in delivering a different amino acid, methionine. This is why eating a grain like rice with beans is a good idea to obtain a complete range of amino acids.

Science and Common Sense

Research can be confusing, too: Recommendations of how best to balance carbohydrates, fats, and proteins in a brain-healthy diet can seem like a roller coaster. As science uncovers new evidence, dietary recommendations for macronutrients will rise and fall to match. That's the nature of science and discovery.

Instead of being swept up in the latest fads, use your brain—as in common sense—to eat right to protect it. Avoid fad diets, quick fixes, and extremes. Seek a sensible balance by embracing the healthy choices we'll explore in the following chapters.

Plants are often overlooked by Americans, but they are powerful suppliers of nutrients, and vegetarian dishes, like this vegetable-rice dish, can be delicious.

How High-Protein Plant Foods Compare to Animal Sources

FOOD	PROTEIN CONTENT (G)
3 oz boneless, skinless chicken breast, cooked	24
6 oz plain Greek yogurt	17
½ cup tempeh	16
½ cup tofu	15
½ cup edamame	10
½ cup lentils	9
½ cup beans, cooked or canned	7-8
2 Tbsp nut butter (peanut, almond, cashew)	6
½ cup green peas (cooked)	5
½ cup quinoa (cooked)	5
1 large egg	4
2 Tbsp pumpkin seeds, roasted	4
12 almonds	3

oz – ounce; Tbsp = tablespoon

Continuing to work your brain and fueling it properly with foods that support brain health are proven ways to help fight cognitive decline.

5 Brain Foods

It's a challenge for science to prove that any specific food helps protect the brain, given the long time it takes to develop conditions such as Alzheimer's disease and other dementias. Most such research on brain-healthy foods or foods that fight memory loss relies on observational studies, in which people who report eating more or less of a certain food are assessed over time for cognitive changes. Such studies are not designed to prove cause and effect, however, only associations. Clinical trials of foods and the brain have often depended on animal tests or small groups of humans.

That's not to say, however, that research hasn't produced some promising results on foods for brain health. For example, a study published Nov. 22, 2022, in *Neurology* reported that flavonols, a phytonutrient found in a wide variety of vegetables as well as fruits, might help protect the aging brain. The study of 961 participants, ages 60-plus, compared flavonol intake with changes in cognitive performance, assessed annually over almost seven years. Higher dietary intake of total flavonols and individual flavonols was associated with a slower rate of decline in global cognition and multiple specific measures of cognition.

Among specific flavonols, intakes of kaempferol and quercetin were associated with slower global cognitive decline. Common foods that contain kaempferol include onions, broccoli, Brussels sprouts, squash, and spinach, as well as apples, grapes, and berries. Quercetin is found in red onions, leafy greens, tomatoes, berries, and other produce.

A study published in *Frontiers in Nutrition* on May 19, 2022, singled out cranberries for possible brain benefits. Scientists tested the cognitive effects of freeze-dried cranberry powder in a 12-week randomized trial with 60 older adults. The daily dosage of cranberry powder (a standard technique in clinical trials to control dosages) was roughly equivalent to consuming one cup of fresh cranberries. Participants, ages 50 to 80, underwent tests of memory and executive function (the mental processes of planning, attention, following instructions, and multitasking), as well as blood tests and neuroimaging. Compared with a control group given a placebo, those in the cranberry group saw improvements in visual episodic memory (the ability to recognize and recall objects) and neural functioning.

Healthy Foods, Not Magic Pills

As these examples suggest, despite the research obstacles, some foods do stand out as most likely being protective for brain health. These "brain foods" typically contain nutrients that scientists believe have positive effects on the brain, either directly or via improved cardiovascular health. Fortunately, these brain-healthy choices are components of a healthy diet, so as you feed your brain, you'll be taking care of the rest of your body.

It's important to keep in mind that these examples of brain foods are not magic pills. Gobbling a handful of blueberries every morning is no substitute for eating right the rest of the day and staying physically active (see "Varied Diet Better for the Brain"). And even brain foods should be consumed in moderation, especially concentrated forms of calories (like nuts and chocolate).

Nutritious Nuts

If you grew up thinking of nuts as an indulgent snack, recent findings suggest it's time for a rethink. Considerable research has shown that nuts are nutritional powerhouses. A comprehensive review of the evidence of health benefits from eating nuts and seeds looked at 89 prior studies and concluded that nuts are associated with reduced risk of cardiovascular diseases. Compared with not eating nuts, an intake of 28 grams per day (a little less than a quarter-cup) was associated with a 21 percent risk reduction.

Other studies have associated frequent nut consumption with lower risks of high blood pressure and insulin resistance. People who increased nut consumption after being diagnosed with diabetes have been found to be less likely to develop cardiovascular disease.

Multiple studies have demonstrated improvements in cholesterol levels and blood-vessel function—also good for your brain—from nut consumption. A Tufts review of 61 prior trials found that nut intake lowered total cholesterol, unhealthy LDL cholesterol, triglycerides, and lipoproteins.

Nuts and Cognition

Studies on specific brain benefits from nut consumption are inconsistent, however, according to a review of 22 prior studies totaling nearly 44,000 participants, though most suggest a protective effect. Overall, the review found that studies targeting populations with a higher risk of cognitive decline tended to report the most favorable results. The most consistent evidence was found for studies involving walnut consumption and cognitive performance: Out of six studies, including two randomized controlled trials, only one did not find a positive association.

Does that mean walnuts are the best choice for your brain? Not necessarily—it could be that walnuts have been more extensively studied, thanks to active and well-funded trade associations.

Results from another trial, the Walnuts and Healthy Aging study, however, were mixed. The two-year intervention involved 708 older adults in California and Spain.

Participants were randomly assigned to either a diet enriched with walnuts (about 15 percent of calories, 30 to 60 grams daily) or a control diet with no walnuts. Healthy adults saw no cognitive benefit from walnut consumption, but scans and tests suggested that walnuts might delay cognitive decline in subgroups at higher risk.

As we've seen, the Spanish PREDIMED study of the Mediterranean diet did

NEW FINDING

Varied Diet Better for the Brain

Older adults who aren't picky eaters may enjoy better mental health and superior cognitive functions relative to those with narrower food choices. Researchers classified almost 182,000 senior participants in the U.K. Biobank study into four dietary subtypes: starch-free or reduced-starch, vegetarian, high-protein and low-fiber, and balanced. The study departed from conventional dietary research by focusing on individuals' food likes and dislikes—rating 140 different foods and beverages—rather than specific diets' health impacts. The analysis, including gray-matter and other brain volumes, found variations by dietary subtype, with some advantages for each. Overall, however, mental scores were highest for the non-picky eaters preferring a balanced diet with the broadest food choices. Researchers said these findings challenge the notion that sticking to a limited diet, such as vegetarian or high-protein regimens, is universally beneficial for overall health.

Nature Mental Health, April 1, 2024

Nutrients in Nuts

Choose whatever variety of nuts you like best, since the nutrient profiles of nuts are more similar than different. Here are some highlights:

- **Almonds** top all tree nuts per ounce in protein, fiber, calcium, vitamin E, niacin, and riboflavin.

- **Brazil nuts** are among the richest dietary sources of selenium and are high in magnesium.

- **Cashews** are the tree nuts highest in iron, copper, and zinc, and are a good source of magnesium.

- **Hazelnuts,** also called filberts, are good sources of vitamin E, manganese, and copper.

- **Macadamia nuts** contain the most calories and fat of all nuts, but most of the fat is of the healthy monounsaturated variety.

- **Peanuts** (technically legumes) are high in fiber, vitamin E, magnesium, folate, and niacin.

- **Pecans** are packed with antioxidants and vitamin E.

- **Pine nuts,** also known as piñon, pinoli, or pignoli, are second only to walnuts in polyunsaturated fat content and provide more than 100 percent of the recommended daily intake of manganese in one serving.

- **Pistachios** have the most potassium and vitamin B_6 and the highest amount of lutein.

- **Walnuts** are the only nut rich in alpha-linolenic acid (ALA), the plant form of omega-3 fatty acids. They are a good source of manganese, copper, magnesium, phosphorus, vitamin B_6, and iron.

report that adding extra nuts seemed to boost protection for aging brains. Those consuming a Mediterranean diet plus an ounce of mixed nuts daily scored better in tests of memory than participants assigned to a control group.

Picking Nuts

Though nuts' nutritional profiles vary, the type of nut you choose to consume probably doesn't matter much. All nuts as well as seeds have plenty of dietary fiber, and they're high in heart-healthy mono- and polyunsaturated fats (including plant omega-3 fatty acids) and low in saturated fats. They also contain many vitamins and minerals, such as vitamin E, magnesium, phosphorus, copper, and manganese.

You might do best by simply eating a variety of nuts, consumed as a substitute for less-healthy snacks. Though peanuts are technically legumes, not tree nuts, their nutrient profile is similar.

All nuts are concentrated sources of calories. Surprisingly, however, eating nuts doesn't appear to be linked to weight gain and might even help control weight. Studies have found that people who eat more nuts don't typically weigh more. That could be because nuts tend to fill you up, leading to a lower consumption of other foods. Even studies where participants simply added nuts to their diets, without eliminating other foods, showed no change in weight.

Berries for the Brain

As we've seen in the MIND diet, there's a good deal of evidence that berries are good for the brain. Tufts researchers have extensively tested berries' brain effects in animals, using powdered berry compounds to simulate the effects of fruit consumption. Compared with rats fed only their normal diet, those consuming diets supplemented with berries had enhanced motor performance and improved cognition. The berries also boosted production of neurons in the hippocampus, possibly improving hippocampus function.

Other Tufts studies found that the addition of blueberries to animals' diets improved short-term memory, navigational skills, balance, coordination, and reaction time. Compounds in blueberries seem to jump-start the brain in ways that get aging neurons to communicate again.

An analysis of data on berry consumption among some 16,000 women over age 70 participating in the Nurses' Health Study suggests how berries might affect aging human brains. The women were tested for cognitive functions every two years and completed dietary questionnaires every four years. Researchers found that those who consumed two or more half-cup servings of strawberries or blueberries per week experienced slower mental decline—equivalent over time to up to 2½ years of delayed aging.

Some data from Alzheimer's patients indicate that blueberries could forestall the brain damage that is a hallmark of the disease. Other berries would likely have similar effects.

Berry Pigments

As with nuts, you can probably choose your favorite berries of any type, confident in their potential brain benefits. Besides blueberries and raspberries, other berries, including strawberries, blackberries, bilberries, huckleberries, and cranberries, as well as grapes and currants, contain similar pigment compounds called anthocyanins. These give berries their distinctive red, purple, and blue colors.

Anthocyanins can cross the blood-brain barrier to become localized in areas of the brain related to learning and memory. In the brain, anthocyanins decrease vulnerability to the oxidative stress that occurs with aging, reduce inflammation, and may increase neuronal signaling.

Grapes, which contain similar pigments, have also been studied for cognitive protection. One trial tested the effects of Concord grape juice versus a placebo beverage in elderly volunteers already suffering from mild cognitive impairment (MCI). After 16 weeks, those who drank grape juice scored better on tests of memory than those in the placebo group. Measurement of brain activity revealed greater activation in the grape-juice group, suggesting increased blood flow in areas of the brain associated with learning and memory.

Eat Your Veggies

Multiple studies have found cardiovascular benefits from adopting a vegetarian or mostly vegetarian diet, so it's not surprising that vegetables and other plant foods may also help protect against strokes. One six-year study of people from Buddhist communities in Taiwan, where a vegetarian diet is encouraged, found that vegetarians were at 74 percent lower risk of stroke than non-vegetarians. Data on a second community similarly found that over an average of nine years, vegetarians had a 48 percent lower risk of overall stroke than non-vegetarians.

Similarly, men participating in the two-decade Health Professionals Follow-Up Study who reported the highest intakes of green leafy vegetables and carotenoid-rich (green, orange, and yellow) vegetables, as well as berry fruits and daily orange juice, had significantly lower odds of moderate and poor self-reported cognitive function compared with those who reported the lowest intakes.

Another study found that two servings a day of vegetables prevented the equivalent of five years of mental aging. Participants who ate at least 2.8 servings of vegetables a day over a span of six years slowed their rate of cognitive decline by about 40 percent compared with those participants who consumed less than one serving a day.

Although "juicing" sacrifices healthy fiber, other nutrients survive to benefit your brain. In a study involving nearly 2,000 older, dementia-free Japanese Americans over nine years, participants who drank at least three glasses of fruit or vegetable juice per week were 76 percent less likely to develop Alzheimer's compared with those who averaged less than one glass per week.

Eating Vitamin E

Spinach, kale, and other leafy greens are high in vitamin E, as are avocados, broccoli, and asparagus. Some animal and observational studies have suggested vitamin E might have a role in the prevention or treatment of Alzheimer's disease.

Because too much vitamin E can be dangerous, however, it's better to get your intake from foods such as vegetables with other health benefits rather than from supplements. It's also worth noting that vegetables are typically consumed with some fats, which increases the absorption of vitamin E and other fat-soluble antioxidant nutrients.

Salad Smarts

When choosing veggies for brain benefits, don't overlook the salad bowl. Leafy green vegetables, such as lettuce, spinach, and kale, might help slow the decline in cognition and memory associated with aging. A prospective study of 960 people, average age 81, assessed participants' diets and thinking and memory ability annually for almost five years. The one-fifth of participants with the greatest average consumption of leafy greens (1.3 daily servings) showed a slower decline than the group eating the least (0.1 daily servings). The difference was the equivalent of a delay of 11 years in cognitive aging, researchers said.

The vegetables included spinach, kale, collards, and other greens (a half cup cooked equals one serving) and lettuce (1 cup raw). Citing two earlier studies, the researchers concluded that "consumption of green leafy vegetables (1 to 2 servings

Organic Shopping Strategy

To save while shopping smart, opt for organic produce when buying the fruits and vegetables most prone to pesticide residue, while buying conventional produce for those found to be "cleanest." The Environmental Working Group (ewg.org) annually ranks the "Dirty Dozen" and "Clean 15" fruits and vegetables, based on testing for pesticide residue.

Here are the **"Dirty Dozen,"** where it pays to buy organic to avoid pesticides:

1. Strawberries
2. Spinach
3. Kale, collard, and mustard greens
4. Grapes
5. Peaches
6. Pears
7. Nectarines
8. Apples
9. Peppers
10. Cherries
11. Blueberries
12. Green beans

And these fruits and vegetables are the **"Clean 15"** that don't need to be purchased as organic produce, if you prefer:

1. Avocados
2. Sweet corn
3. Pineapple
4. Onions
5. Papaya
6. Sweet peas (frozen)
7. Asparagus
8. Honeydew melon
9. Kiwi
10. Cabbage
11. Mushrooms
12. Mangoes
13. Sweet potatoes
14. Watermelon
15. Carrots

> **Keeping Salads Safe**
>
> Though packed with brain-beneficial nutrients, salad greens can also contain bacterial contaminants that can cause foodborne illness. Keep in mind these safety tips:
>
> - At the market, place fresh greens in plastic bags to keep them separate from raw meats and poultry.
> - Refrigerate greens at 35 to 40 degrees.
> - Wash hands and surfaces before preparing salad.
> - Wash all non-prewashed greens thoroughly under running water just before using, including produce grown at home and/or purchased from a grocery store or farmers market.
> - If the label on packaged greens indicates that the contents are pre-washed and ready to eat, the FDA says you can use the produce without further washing.

per day) and foods rich in phylloquinone (vitamin K), lutein, nitrate, folate, alpha-tocopherol (vitamin E), and kaempferol (a flavonoid) may slow decline in cognitive abilities with older age."

Omega-3s from the Sea

The American Heart Association (AHA) recommends eating fish at least two times a week; one serving is 3.5 ounces cooked, or about three-quarters of a cup of flaked fish. Fish species that are especially high in omega-3s include salmon, anchovies, and Atlantic and Pacific mackerel, according to the AHA.

A comprehensive review of meta-analyses found moderate-quality evidence for a benefit of fish consumption against cardiovascular mortality, coronary heart disease, stroke, and depression, among other benefits. Each additional 100 grams (about 3.5 ounces) per day of fish consumption was associated with a 14 percent lower risk of stroke and a 12 percent lower risk of depression.

Fish for Brain Health

The importance of omega-3s—in particular, DHA—to seafood's cognitive effects was demonstrated in a Tufts study several years ago. It involved nearly 900 elderly adults initially free of dementia who were screened for cognitive decline every two years; 488 participants also completed a dietary questionnaire. Those with the highest blood DHA levels ate an average of nearly three fish servings a week. Following up an average of nine years later, researchers found that participants with higher blood levels of DHA, as well as those eating the most fish, had a dramatically lower risk of dementia and Alzheimer's disease. Subjects with the highest DHA levels had a 47 percent reduced risk of dementia and a 39 percent lower risk of Alzheimer's.

A 2022 study published in *Cureus* found that the brains of people with high blood levels of seafood omega-3s showed greater blood flow in brain areas involved in memory and learning. This group also scored higher on tests of cognitive function than people with lower levels of omega-3s.

Last year we also saw an observational study that reported eating fish may help prevent brain damage from cerebrovascular disease. Published in *Neurology*, the study looked at 1,623 participants in the Three-City Dijon study, average age 72.3. Participants, who were initially free of dementia, stroke, or hospitalized cardiovascular disease, underwent an MRI brain scan and reported their fish intake.

Higher fish consumption—eating fish twice a week or more—was associated with healthier brain condition, such as fewer white-matter hypersensitivities and infarcts, compared with eating fish less than once a week. The protective association was strongest among younger participants (ages 65 to 69). In this group, the beneficial effect of eating fish two to three times a week was roughly equivalent to the negative effects of hypertension (in the opposite direction).

Even if you've never been a big seafood eater, it's not too late to reduce your risk of cognitive impairment by eating more fish. It may even be more beneficial later in life. Chinese researchers reported that age significantly modified the association between fish consumption and cognitive change. Among adults ages 65 and older, those who ate one or more servings of fish weekly saw a slower rate of cognitive decline compared with those consuming less fish. The difference was equivalent to what would be expected from 1.6 years of difference in age. Fish consumption also was associated with a slower decline in composite and verbal memory scores. No associations were observed among those ages 55 to 64.

Preparation Matters

How you prepare seafood makes a difference in obtaining its apparent brain benefits. In a study using MRI scans, people eating broiled or baked fish—not fried fish—on a weekly basis had greater volumes of gray matter in the brain's hippocampus and frontal and temporal lobes.

That's not the only study to find that consuming baked and broiled (or microwaved, grilled, or poached) fish is more beneficial than eating fried fish. Some studies have even shown that deep frying damages omega-3 fats.

The type of fish commonly used for frying also may be a factor: Cod and other ocean whitefish varieties are much lower in omega-3 content than other fish.

Shellfish choices fall a bit short on omega-3s, too. Although shrimp, for example, is a lean source of high-quality protein, it is low in total fat and thus also low in omega-3 fatty acids. The omega-3 content of crab is somewhat higher, similar to that of canned light tuna, although it varies widely by species.

Dark Chocolate Findings

Cocoa beans contain dozens of different phytonutrients—plant compounds that have biological, often health-promoting, effects in humans. Among these are flavonols found in dark chocolate—the darker, the better—and cocoa.

Cocoa-bean flavanols are associated with improvements in blood pressure, blood glucose, and insulin resistance. It isn't clear whether the benefits in cognition seen in some studies are a direct consequence of cocoa flavanols or a secondary effect of these general improvements in health.

Chocolate Research

Some studies have tried to factor out those issues. The Maine-Syracuse Longitudinal Study looked at habitual chocolate consumption and cognition in 968 participants ages 23 to 98. It found that more frequent chocolate consumption was significantly associated with better performance on cognitive tests, even after scientists controlled for cardiovascular, lifestyle, and dietary variables.

A study conducted in Spain reported that older adults who habitually consumed at least 10 grams, which is less than a half ounce, of any type of chocolate per day had better cognitive function than those who did not eat chocolate. Dark chocolate consumption was associated with a lower likelihood of mild cognitive impairment.

Effects on Impairment. People who have already suffered cognitive impairment might also get a boost from chocolate. In one Italian clinical trial, older adults with mild cognitive impairment improved their scores on some mental tests when they consumed cocoa flavanols. Importantly, researchers noted, the improvements in cognitive function were seen over a relatively short period of time—just eight weeks.

Chronic Conditions. Another study tested the effects of cocoa consumption in 60 volunteers, average age 73, who had hypertension and/or diabetes. Although none had dementia, 17 suffered from impaired neurovascular coupling (NVC), a measure of blood flow in the brain as it relates to nerve cells (neurons). Participants free of impaired NVC showed no significant benefits from cocoa consumption. But the small group of volunteers with impaired NVC saw dramatic changes after just a month of cocoa intake: NVC improved by more than double, and scores on standard cognitive tests jumped 30 percent.

No food can make you immune to dementia. An overall healthy dietary pattern can reduce your risk and protect your brain power just as a healthy diet can help protect your heart.

Shopping for Omega-3s

According to the FDA and EPA, these fish are the best choices for avoiding mercury contamination, while also being highest in omega-3 fatty acids. You can eat these two to three times a week:

- Anchovy
- Atlantic mackerel
- Herring
- Salmon
- Sardine
- Shad
- Trout (freshwater)
- Whitefish (lake)

These fish high in omega-3s are good choices, suitable for eating once a week:

- Bluefish
- Halibut
- Sablefish
- Spanish mackerel
- Striped bass (ocean)
- Tilefish (Atlantic)
- Tuna, albacore/"white" (fresh, frozen, or canned)
- Tuna, yellowfin

Not all these choices are equally sustainable. For the latest on sustainable seafood choices, see the Monterey Bay Aquarium's Seafood Watch at seafoodwatch.org.

Hydration is critical to life, and many things we consume, including coffee (now considered healthy!), add to our daily fluid intake.

6 Healthy Beverage Choices

About 75 percent of your brain is water, so it makes sense that staying hydrated is important for maintaining cognitive function. Water is involved in many critical bodily functions, from maintaining blood pressure and transporting nutrients to lubricating joints, digesting foods, removing waste from the body, and regulating body temperature.

Your body loses fluids through sweating and urination, and, if sick, also through vomiting, diarrhea, or blood loss. If you lose significantly more fluids than you take in, the result is dehydration. Besides endangering your body, chronic dehydration can contribute to fatigue and reduced mental activity. Dehydration also can place stress on the cardiovascular system, which in turn affects the brain.

One analysis of 33 studies found that attention, coordination, and complex problem-solving suffer the most from dehydration. Scientists looked at the records of people who lost fluids amounting to 1 to 6 percent of their body mass either through exercise, exposure to heat, or fluid restriction. Severe impairments started at 2 percent, a level that has been a significant benchmark in related studies. For a 160-pound person, that's a little over 3 pounds of water, which could be lost in just a few hours of moderately intense activity in the heat.

Eight Glasses vs. Thirst

In generally healthy people, following the rule to "obey your thirst" is enough to maintain adequate hydration for a healthy cardiovascular system and brain. But with aging, the body's ability to sense hydration and thirst may be less sensitive. Several studies suggest that older adults drink less water than younger adults, although they need just as much in general.

You may also have heard that everyone should drink eight 8-ounce glasses of water daily. Although this is not a bad rule of thumb, it's not strictly true—nor is it supported by science. How much fluid a person needs for hydration depends on many factors, including body size, physical activity level, ambient temperature, humidity, and altitude. If you are playing pickleball on a hot day, for example, you will need more water than if you are quietly reading in an air-conditioned room.

According to the National Academy of Science, 15.5 cups of water intake for most men and 11.5 cups for most women per day is adequate (more for women who are pregnant or lactating). This is much higher than the eight 8-ounce cup standard, but foods (such as fruits, vegetables, soup, and even fish, eggs, meat, and cooked grains) supply a significant part of your fluid needs. Beverages like coffee, tea, and milk contribute fluids—and, yes, caffeinated beverages count. Caffeine can modestly increase water loss through urination, but not enough to cause dehydration. This effect may be less prominent in people who habitually drink caffeinated drinks like coffee or tea.

Yes, Coffee Counts

Not only does that morning cup of coffee count toward your daily hydration needs, it also contains phytonutrients that benefit your heart and brain. Scientists now view coffee, as well as tea, as a sort of plant food—with brain benefits like those from other plant sources of phytonutrients.

A study published in *Nutrition Research* in January 2023 reported that caffeine is positively associated with cognitive performance, especially in older men. Researchers analyzed data on 827 individuals, ages 60 and up, from the National Health and Nutrition Examination Surveys (NHANES). The study compared cognitive performance on two standard tests with urinary caffeine amounts and 14 different markers of caffeine metabolism. As measures of caffeine increased, so did cognitive scores; the positive association was strongest among male participants. The study did not differentiate between dietary sources of caffeine, such as coffee and tea.

Last year, in a study published in *Frontiers in Aging Neuroscience*, we saw evidence that coffee may protect against Alzheimer's disease and help slow cognitive decline. The Australian study followed 227 older adults, initially cognitively normal, for more than 10 years. Scientists investigated the relationship between coffee intake and cognitive decline, using a comprehensive neuropsychological battery of tests. A subgroup of participants was also analyzed for brain volume and buildup of the amyloid compounds characteristic of Alzheimer's.

Higher coffee consumption at the study's start was associated with a slower decline in executive function, attention, and composite cognitive score. Higher consumption was also associated with slower amyloid accumulation and lower risk of progressing to worse amyloid status.

Tapping Into Water

In most U.S. cities, ordinary tap water is among the safest fluid sources you can choose. Tap water from public water systems is regulated by the Environmental Protection Agency (EPA). Routine testing of public water is required, and test results must be made available to the public. Although there may be headline-making local exceptions, U.S. drinking water is among the safest and most reliable in the world.

Nonetheless, bottled waters are now the No. 1 beverage in the United States. These products come at a cost—both financial and environmental—so knowing what you're getting and weighing your options carefully is important.

These steps can help you become water-wise:

- Carry a reusable water bottle.
- Read labels on flavored waters, as some have added sugars.
- Don't believe unverified health claims about specialty waters like alkaline and electrolyte products.
- If you have concerns about your municipal or well water supply, invest in a water filter (whole-house, under-sink, refrigerator, or pitcher) and replace all filters as recommended.

Be aware that many bottled drinking waters come from a municipal source, just like tap water.

Calories Lurk in Lattes

Drinking your coffee black, without creamers and sugars, can save you an average of 69 calories per cup. You may not give much thought to adding a splash of cream and a spoonful of sugar to your coffee or tea, or to all the extras in lattes, but these add-ins can add up.

Coffee offers a multitude of healthy benefits, as well as being a somewhat soothing choice.

Coffee Combats Depression

Drinking coffee also could help ward off depression. A Harvard study reported that women consuming two or three cups of regular coffee per day were 15 percent less likely to develop depression over a follow-up period of 10 years than those drinking one cup a day or less. Those drinking four cups a day were at 20 percent lower risk.

Before you go overboard at your local coffee shop, however, remember calories. Black coffee is basically zero-calorie, but things change if you add cream, milk, sugar, and more.

Tea: Drinking Plants

Tea, like coffee, contains caffeine and comes from plants rich in helpful phytonutrients. Tea drinkers have been shown to have 20 times higher flavonoid intake than non-consumers; about one-third of the weight of a tea leaf is flavonoids.

All tea comes from the leaves of the *Camellia sinensis* bush. Green tea is unfermented and minimally processed; the leaves are simply withered and steamed. Black tea is fermented and oxidized. Oolong tea is partly oxidized, between green and black tea. White tea is made from partly opened buds and young leaves, which are steamed and dried. Herbal tea, while not made from tea leaves, also may have health benefits.

Focus on Green Tea

Among these varieties, the most cognitive-specific science has focused on green tea, which is rich in a polyphenol called EGCG (epigallocatechin-3-gallate). Researchers found that EGCG prevents the formation of potentially dangerous amyloid aggregates associated with the development of Alzheimer's disease. A green-tea extract also broke down aggregates in proteins that contained metals—copper, iron, and zinc—associated with the disease.

British scientists tested the effect of green tea extracts on amyloid proteins created in the lab. The extracts caused the shape of the balls to distort in such a way that they could no longer bind to nerve cells and disrupt their functioning.

One small clinical trial reported that green tea improves the connectivity between parts of the brain involved in tasks of working memory. In another study, looking at people with mild memory impairment, daily supplements of green tea extract plus L-theanine (an amino acid unique to tea) over four months improved memory and mental alertness compared to a placebo.

Tea and Hypertension

Tea also seems to have a beneficial effect on high blood pressure, the No.1 risk factor for strokes and vascular dementia. An Australian study reported that drinking three cups daily of regular black tea was associated with a small but significant drop in blood pressure compared to a placebo beverage containing the same amount of caffeine but no tea.

A Chinese study of nearly 490,000 people looked at tea consumption and the risk of stroke over an average of nine years of follow-up. Overall, as self-reported tea consumption increased, the risk of stroke went down.

Hibiscus and High Blood Pressure. Though not technically "tea," herbal teas also possess plant power and may have similar blood-pressure benefits. Hibiscus is one of the most common ingredients in herbal teas. It gives the beverages a fruity, tart taste and red color. This fruit of a flowering plant is rich in antioxidants including anthocyanins, flavones, flavonols, and phenolic acids.

Tufts University research led by Diane L. McKay, PhD, showed that a few cups a day of herbal tea containing hibiscus can help lower high blood pressure in prehypertensive and mildly hypertensive adults as effectively as some medications. In one such study, those who drank hibiscus tea saw a 7.2-point drop in their systolic blood pressure, significantly more than a placebo group. Participants with the highest blood pressure at the study's start showed the most significant reductions.

Coffee and Tea Brain Benefits

Other research has looked at brain benefits from both coffee and tea. An eight-year study of nearly 14,000 older Japanese, published in the *Journal of the American Geriatrics Society*, reported that high levels of coffee and caffeine consumption were significantly associated with a reduced dementia risk, especially in men. Notably, as intake increased, risk fell—what's known as a "dose-dependent" association. Coffee consumption of three or more cups a day was linked to a 50 percent reduction in dementia risk, compared to the lowest one-fifth of consumption. Green tea consumption was also associated with reduced dementia risk, but only among those ages 60 to 69.

Another study, published in *PLOS Medicine*, found that drinking coffee and tea, separately or in combination, may help protect against stroke and dementia. Drinking coffee alone or with tea also might reduce the risk of post-stroke dementia. Researchers analyzed data on more than 365,000 participants, ages 50 to 74, from the U.K. Biobank study.

The lowest risk of incident stroke and dementia was associated with coffee intake of two to three cups daily, tea intake of three to five cups daily, or combined consumption of four to six cups a day. Compared with those who didn't drink tea or coffee, drinking two to three daily cups of either beverage was associated with a 32 percent lower stroke risk and 28 percent lower dementia risk.

These findings align well with earlier results from the Baltimore Longitudinal Study of Aging, which showed that caffeine intake was associated with better baseline global cognition among participants ages 70 and older.

Packaged Beverages

Although bottled water is now Americans' No. 1 beverage, we still drink plenty of sodas and other bottled and canned beverages. Drinks with lots of added sugars, like sodas, energy drinks, sports drinks, sweetened ice teas, coffee drinks, and fruit drinks, may quench your thirst, but plenty of evidence shows that they are bad for your health. Even 100 percent fruit juice provides a dose of natural sugar that could add unneeded calories without the fiber naturally present in fruit (most guidelines recommend no more than one 8-ounce serving of fruit juice each day).

What about diet sodas? The health effects of low-calorie or zero-calorie drinks that use artificial or naturally low-calorie sweeteners remain controversial. While there is no strong evidence of harm, growing signals from animal studies and some research in humans suggest these may not be as safe as water. Those concerns include effects on cognition.

Some studies have raised the possibility that there is an association between the consumption of artificially sweetened beverages and an increased risk for dementia and stroke. One study found that women ages 50 and older who drank 24 or more ounces of diet soda a day were 23 percent more likely to have a stroke than those who drank less than 12 ounces a week, but more research is needed.

A 10-year study of participants in the Framingham Heart Study reported that those who drank diet soda daily were almost three times as likely to suffer a stroke and develop dementia as those who consumed it weekly or less. Participants consumed artificial sweeteners including saccharin, acesulfame-K (ace-K), and aspartame; however, more newer

© Showface | Dreamstime

Energy drinks can be hydrating, but watch the calories and sugar contents and don't overdo your consumption of them.

Energy Drinks: Caffeine and Calories

Promising a quick pick-me-up, energy drinks have soared in popularity in recent years. The most common ingredients in these drinks are caffeine, sugar, B vitamins, and amino acids. Although both caffeine and sugar can give you a short-term jolt, there are safer ways to obtain caffeine, and sugar just adds calories.

Without caffeine, these energy drinks have little effect. Researchers compared a decaffeinated energy drink with a placebo beverage among 223 healthy adults, ages 18 to 70. No statistically significant benefits were observed for the energy drinks on any outcome measure, including mood and cognitive measures.

While science battles out the question about whether red wine is good for you or not, use the age-old advice of "everything in moderation."

sweeteners, such as sucralose, neotame, and stevia, were not included.

Reaching for an occasional diet soda probably won't put your cognition at risk. But the go-to drink for a healthy brain is still plain water.

Updates on Alcohol

Scientific opinion on the health effects of alcohol consumption has lately turned sharply negative. Even the notion of a glass of red wine being good for the heart has fallen out of favor.

A study from the *Journal of the American Medical Association*, published in March 2022, involved over 300,000 participants in their mid-50s who consumed alcohol. The study found any amount of alcohol was linked with a higher risk of cardiovascular disease than consuming no alcohol, and the higher the use of alcohol, the higher the risk of cardiovascular disease.

Brain Effects

As with other aspects of health, the evidence for the effects of alcohol on cognition is mixed to negative. Last year we saw a study in *Nature Communications* that concluded even light-to-moderate alcohol consumption—one or two drinks a day—might be associated with lower overall brain volume. The analysis of nearly 37,000 healthy adults in the U.K. Biobank study found that alcohol intake was negatively associated with global brain volume measures, regional gray matter volumes, and white matter microstructure. As consumption increased, the link to lower brain volumes strengthened.

Even increasing from one alcohol "unit" per day (half a beer or glass of wine) to two units was associated with brain changes in 50-year-olds equivalent to two years of additional aging. Going from two to three units daily was linked to the equivalent of 3.5 years of brain aging. Even when the heaviest drinkers were excluded from the data, the associations between alcohol and brain aging remained.

Similarly, a meta-analysis found each additional drink per week was associated with nearly 4 percent higher risk of developing mild cognitive impairment (MCI). Heavy alcohol intake (defined in this study as more than 14 drinks per week) was associated with higher risk of progression from MCI to dementia.

Is Moderate Drinking OK? On the other hand, a study that tracked cognitive performance over 10 years did report that light-to-moderate drinking may preserve brain function in older age. Nearly 20,000 people completed surveys every two years about their health and lifestyle, including questions about drinking habits. Light-to-moderate drinking was defined as fewer than eight drinks per week for women and 15 drinks or fewer per week among men. Compared with non-drinkers, those who had a drink or two a day tended to perform better on cognitive tests over time. The optimal number of drinks per week was between 10 and 14. But that doesn't mean those who drink less should start indulging more, researchers cautioned, or that non-drinkers should take up drinking.

Another study that followed nearly 20,000 middle-aged or older participants for nine years found that low-to-moderate alcohol intake (compared with never drinking) was associated with higher cognitive scores and lower rates of cognitive decline.

Goldilocks Drinking. Still other research suggests that a "Goldilocks effect" might apply to alcohol and the brain, with a "just right" amount of drinking associated with reduced dementia risk. A large prospective study of more than 9,000 individuals over 23 years concluded that too much—or too little—alcohol consumption was associated with greater risk of dementia.

The study found that people who consumed one to 14 standard drinks per week were at the lowest risk of dementia.

Compared with moderate drinkers, those who abstained completely were at 47 percent greater risk. Overdoing alcohol had its own downsides, however, as every seven-drink increase in weekly consumption was linked to a 17 percent greater dementia risk. People with a high score on a measure of alcohol dependence saw more than twice the rate of dementia.

Alcohol and Alzheimer's. What about the effects of alcohol consumption on Alzheimer's disease risk? Some research has linked moderate drinking to lower levels of the protein that forms brain plaques in Alzheimer's disease. Moderate alcohol consumption—but not heavy drinking—might help lower levels of beta-amyloid, the protein that forms the brain plaques of Alzheimer's disease.

A Korean study of more than 400 older adults, initially free of dementia or alcohol-related disorders, compared drinking habits with clinical testing, including brain scans. Compared with abstainers, those who consumed up to 13 drinks per week had a 66 percent lower level of beta-amyloid deposits in their brains. People who consumed more than 13 drinks a week or who had only recently begun moderate drinking did not have lower beta-amyloid levels.

Researching Red Wine. Red wine is often singled out for potential health benefits. It contains bioactive compounds called polyphenols that have been associated with cardiovascular health. In the 1990s and early 2000s, a slew of observational studies supported the idea that red wine, in particular, was protective. Subsequent analyses, however, raised questions about these findings: Might red wine lovers be wealthier and healthier in other ways? Could the ranks of nonrinkers include former heavy imbibers whose health had already been damaged?

More recent research shows that even one drink per day can increase your chances of developing conditions like high blood pressure and irregular heart rhythms. A 2023 study in *JAMA Network Open* found no link between alcohol consumption and reduced mortality risk.

What About Cognitive Effects? Scientists have shown that the polyphenols in red wine block the formation of proteins that contribute to the development of the toxic brain plaques associated with Alzheimer's disease. These red-wine compounds also reduce the toxicity of existing plaques. Natural chemicals found in red wine (like those in green tea) can interrupt the process by which Alzheimer's proteins latch onto brain cells.

Given health concerns about alcohol, however, keep in mind that all the potentially beneficial compounds in red wine are also found in other foods and beverages. For example, flavonoids, which account for over 85 percent of the polyphenols in red wine, are common in many vegetables, seeds, nuts, spices, and herbs. Resveratrol, a much-hyped compound being studied for health benefits, is found in grape skins and wine, but also in more than 70 other plant species, including berries, peanuts, and cocoa.

Like all alcoholic beverages, wine should be consumed only in moderation, no more than two glasses a day for men and one for women—and even those long-standing recommendations may be too high. If you don't currently drink, the mixed evidence on alcohol and cognition should not inspire you to start.

Much of the research on brain-boosting beverages—such as coffee, tea, and possibly red wine—stems from the plant-derived nutrients they contain. In the next chapter, we'll zoom in on these to explore how and whether they might benefit your heart and brain.

Measuring One Drink

What counts as one drink of an alcoholic beverage? The answer is probably less than you think—or typically pour. According to the Centers for Disease Control and Prevention, one drink is equivalent to:

- **12 ounces of beer** (5% alcohol content)
- **8 ounces of malt liquor** (7% alcohol content)
- **5 ounces of wine** (12% alcohol content)
- **1.5 ounces of 80-proof** (40% alcohol content) distilled spirits or liquor

Nutrition powerhouses are found more in fruits and vegetables than any other food.

7 Nutrients For Heart and Brain

In previous chapters, we've looked at the cognitive effects of macronutrients and at specific foods that might have brain benefits. Drilling down another level, recent studies suggest that individual vitamins, minerals, and phytonutrients found in such foods can help protect your aging brain. Given the evidence for health benefits from plant foods, the case for positive brain effects from individual nutrients found in these foods is among the most encouraging.

For example, a study in the March 10, 2023, *European Journal of Nutrition* identified another potentially important nutrient for cognitive protection, particularly among women: magnesium. The study of more than 6,000 U.K. Biobank participants, ages 40 to 73, used questionnaires to estimate dietary magnesium intake five times over a 16-month span. Examples of foods that were assessed and contained higher magnesium levels included leafy green vegetables such as spinach, legumes, nuts, seeds, and whole grains. On average, higher dietary magnesium intake was strongly associated with larger brain volumes, including gray matter and left and right hippocampus, in both men and women. Although magnesium can help maintain healthy blood-pressure levels—also beneficial to the brain—better blood pressure did not appear to be the driving factor in the effects of magnesium on brain volume.

Choline, found in foods including liver, eggs, beef, chicken, fish, and broccoli, might help protect the aging brain. In a study published November 2022 in the *American Journal of Clinical Nutrition*, scientists used data on 3,224 participants in the Framingham Heart Study Offspring Cohort Exam. Participants, initially free of dementia and stroke, completed a 126-item food-frequency questionnaire. Over an average of 16 years, 247 participants developed dementia, with 177 of those developing Alzheimer's disease. Low choline intake was significantly associated with an increased risk of incident dementia and Alzheimer's disease.

We'll look in-depth at the importance of getting enough vitamin D later in this chapter, but another recent study is worth spotlighting: Published in the August 2022 *American Journal of Clinical Nutrition*,

42 | Special Report

the findings also used data from the U.K. Biobank study. Among the more than 427,000 participants, vitamin D deficiency was associated with an increased risk of dementia and stroke. The strongest associations were seen for those with blood levels of vitamin D below 25 nanomoles per liter (nmol/L): They had a 79 percent greater risk than for those with levels of 50–76 nmol/L. (In adults, deficiency is defined as levels below 25 nmol/L.) A similar risk association for dementia, but not stroke, was seen among more than 33,000 participants who underwent neuroimaging scans. Scientists calculated that 17 percent of dementia cases could be prevented by increasing vitamin D levels from 25 nmol/L to 50 nmol/L.

Plant Power

Less familiar nutrients with heart and brain benefits include a wide variety of phytonutrient compounds such as flavonoids. Last year, we learned that long-term consumption of flavonoid-rich foods is associated with a reduced risk of cognitive decline. Published in *Neurology*, that research used data from two long-running studies of health professionals, totaling more than 77,000 participants.

The intake of flavonoids, plant pigments found in many fruits and vegetables and plant-derived foods, was calculated from up to seven repeated dietary questionnaires per person. Cognitive decline was based on self-assessments over 14 to 22 years. Higher intake was associated with lower odds of cognitive decline. A dose-response relationship (more intake, lower decline) was strongest for flavones, followed by anthocyanins. Many specific flavonoid-rich foods, such as strawberries, oranges, grapefruits, citrus juices, apples, pears, celery, peppers, and bananas, were significantly associated with lower odds of cognitive decline.

Another study, in the *American Journal of Clinical Nutrition*, reported that foods rich in flavonoids have anti-inflammatory and other properties that may decrease the risk of the most common type of stroke. The analysis of more than 55,000 initially stroke-free participants, average age 56, in the Danish Diet, Cancer, and Health Study compared estimated habitual flavonoid intake with ischemic stroke incidence over 21 years. During that span, 4,237 participants suffered an ischemic stroke. Those in the one-fifth of greatest flavonoid intake were 12 percent less likely to suffer a stroke. Consumption of a group of flavonoids such as the tannins in tea was linked to an 18 percent lower risk. Anthocyanins, such as those in berries, were also associated with lower risk.

Flavonol Findings. Another study reported that people who eat or drink more foods with flavonols, a type of flavonoid found in nearly all fruits and vegetables as well as tea, may be less likely to develop Alzheimer's years later. Researchers followed 921 initially non-demented people, average age 81, for more than six years. Higher total intake of flavonols was linked to a 48 percent lower risk of Alzheimer's. Those with the highest intake of a flavonol called kaempferol, primarily from kale, beans, tea, spinach, and broccoli, showed a 51 percent lower rate of developing Alzheimer's than those with the lowest intake.

Two other flavonols were each associated with a 38 percent lower risk: isorhamnetin from pears, olive oil, wine, and tomato sauce; and myricetin from tea, wine, kale, oranges, and tomatoes.

Flavonoids vs. Dementia. Another study of flavonoids used data from the long-running Framingham Heart Study Offspring Cohort. Scientists compared flavonoid intake across five exams with Alzheimer's development over almost 20 years among 2,801 participants, initially an average of 59 years old. Participants with the highest intake of flavonols,

---

The Facts on Flavonoids

A type of phytonutrient, flavonoids are a large family of plant compounds that seem to have various health benefits, including cognitive. Dietary flavonoids naturally occur in fruits, vegetables, chocolate, and beverages like wine and tea. Six major subclasses of flavonoids are the most widespread in the human diet and most studied for health effects:

- **Anthocyanidins/anthocyanins:** Found in red, blue, and purple berries and grapes, and red wine
- **Flavan-3-ols:** Tea, cocoa and chocolate, berries, grapes, apples
- **Flavonols:** Onions, scallions, kale, broccoli, apples, berries, tea
- **Flavones:** Hot peppers, parsley, thyme, celery
- **Flavanones:** Citrus fruit and juices
- **Isoflavones:** Soy foods, legumes

Foods High in Antioxidants

Vitamin C
- Citrus fruits (such as oranges and grapefruit)
- Other fruits and vegetables—such as broccoli, strawberries, cantaloupe, baked potatoes, red and green peppers, kiwifruit, and tomatoes
- Vitamin C-fortified foods

Vitamin E
- Vegetable oils like sunflower and safflower oils are among the best sources; corn and soybean oils also provide some vitamin E
- Nuts (such as peanuts, hazelnuts, and, especially, almonds) and seeds
- Green vegetables, such as spinach and broccoli
- Some fortified breakfast cereals, fruit juices, margarines, spreads, and other foods; check labels

Beta-carotene
- Green leafy vegetables and other green, orange, and yellow vegetables, such as broccoli, carrots, and squash
- Fruits, especially orange-fleshed fruits such as cantaloupe, apricots, and mangos

Selenium
- Seafood
- Meat, poultry, eggs, and dairy products
- Brazil nuts
- Breads, cereals, and other grain products

Zinc
- Oysters, red meat, poultry, other seafood
- Fortified breakfast cereals
- Beans, nuts, whole grains, and dairy products

Source: National Institutes of Health Office of Dietary Supplements

anthocyanins, and other flavonoids had a lower risk than those with the lowest intakes. Anthocyanins, a plant pigment found in berries and other produce, were most strongly associated with lower risk, with participants consuming the most at 76 percent lower risk compared with the lowest-intake group.

Exploring Antioxidants

Many phytonutrients also function as antioxidants. Almost every group of flavonoids, for example, has a capacity to act as antioxidants. That term also covers familiar nutrients such as vitamins C and E, carotenoids such as beta-carotene, and the minerals selenium and zinc. Antioxidants are so called because they scavenge natural byproducts of the body's use of oxygen, called free radicals. Antioxidants reduce oxidative stress and damage to cellular DNA—including cells in the brain.

Antioxidant-rich foods benefit your health, and antioxidant nutrients may help counter chronic disease. As our understanding of these effects grows, scientists have focused more broadly on these compounds' effects—including their ability to counter free radicals.

Antioxidant Evidence

The evidence for antioxidants' benefits for the brain is mixed, particularly when focused on more familiar antioxidants. Another study reported that higher exposure to vitamin C, beta-carotene, vitamin A, or urate (a compound of uric acid) did not lower Alzheimer's risk. Researchers compared antioxidant concentrations in 17,008 late-onset cases of Alzheimer's disease with 37,154 controls who did not develop the disease. No significant association was seen.

A review of the evidence of how antioxidant nutrients affect cognitive performance narrowed 850 eligible studies down to the 10 best studies.

The most convincing evidence, scientists concluded, involved blood levels of selenium and the intake of vitamins C, E, and carotenes—but mostly from dietary sources. A decrease in selenium levels in the blood over nine years was associated with an accelerated decline in global cognition, attention, and psychomotor speed. People in the highest one-fifth of intake of vitamins C, E, and carotenes saw a slower rate of global cognitive decline over three years.

Antioxidants in Pills

Other studies have explored whether supplements of these beneficial compounds might have similar protective effects. To date, there is no reason to switch from fruits and vegetables to supplements. And since the mechanisms of the protective effects of fruits and vegetables on the brain have not been fully explained, the only way to be sure to experience them is by consuming foods instead of pills.

A 2019 study by Tufts University researchers found that a higher intake of certain vitamins and minerals, such as vitamin A, vitamin K, magnesium, zinc, and copper, was associated with a lower risk of death when these nutrients came from food, not supplements. Researchers also reported that excess nutrient intake could have adverse effects.

A panel of World Health Organization (WHO) experts concluded: "There is currently no evidence to show that taking these supplements reduces the risk of cognitive decline and dementia, and in fact, we know that in high doses these can be harmful."

Carotenoids for Cognition

You're probably already eating foods rich in another group of antioxidants being studied for cognitive benefits—carotenoids. These mostly yellow, orange, or red fat-soluble plant pigments are responsible for colors ranging from red tomatoes to autumn leaves. The most familiar carotenoid is beta-carotene, found in foods ranging from carrots (hence the terms *carotene* and *carotenoid*) to leafy greens. Beta-carotene is converted by the body into vitamin A; other vitamin A precursor carotenoids are alpha-carotene and beta-cryptoxanthin.

Lutein, zeaxanthin, and lycopene are called non-provitamin-A carotenoids because, despite their health benefits, they can't be converted into vitamin A. Lutein and zeaxanthin are found in leafy greens, corn, peppers, avocado, and other produce; they form important pigments in the macula of the eye. Lycopene gives foods such as tomatoes, watermelon, and guava their red and pink colors. Importantly, lutein, zeaxanthin, and lycopene are the only carotenoids that cross the blood-retina barrier and accumulate in the human brain.

Studying Carotenoids

Testing blood levels of carotenoids may give a good picture of these compounds' cognitive-protection effects. In a study published May 22, 2022, in *Neurology*, scientists who analyzed data on 7,283 participants in a national health and nutrition survey suggested that their method and findings "might explain why results from dietary comparison studies for the development of dementia have been mixed." Participants were followed for 16 to 17 years using Medicare and Medicaid data. Among those 65 and older, levels of lutein plus zeaxanthin were associated with reduced dementia risk. As levels of another carotenoid, beta-cryptoxanthin, increased, dementia risk fell. No similar associations were found for lycopene, alpha-carotene, beta-carotene, or vitamins A, C, or E, although some seemed to have protective effects when levels of other antioxidants were low.

In another study, researchers looked at data on 927 participants from the Rush Memory and Aging Project who were initially free from Alzheimer's and were followed for about seven years. Among 508 participants who died, postmortem brain autopsies assessed neuropathology associated with Alzheimer's. Higher intake of total carotenoids was associated with substantially lower Alzheimer's risk after controlling for other factors. Comparing the top and bottom one-fifth of carotenoid intake, risk of developing the disease for those consuming the most was roughly half. A similar association was observed for lutein and zeaxanthin. Among deceased participants, consumers of higher total carotenoids showed fewer signs of Alzheimer's; lutein, zeaxanthin, and lycopene specifically were inversely associated with brain pathology.

Intervention Trials. Other research tested giving carotenoids to individuals in food or pill form. In a small randomized, controlled trial of 49 older women, supplementation with 12 milligrams of lutein over four months was associated with significantly higher scores on cognitive function tests for verbal fluency. Memory scores and rate of learning improved significantly when lutein was paired with the omega-3 fatty acid DHA.

A subsequent intervention trial compared a lutein-enhanced diet (in the form of avocado) with a diet containing the same number of calories but no additional lutein. After six months, the researchers found significant increases in macular pigment (a measure of lutein in the retina and a biomarker of lutein in the brain), along with improvements in problem-solving and other brain functions, in the lutein group of participants.

Another small trial, involving supplements of lutein and zeaxanthin among 44 older adults, reported that the compounds appear to benefit neurocognitive function by enhancing blood flow to the brain. After one year, supplementation appeared to slow cognitive decline on a test of verbal learning, and functional magnetic resonance imaging (fMRI) scans showed significant increases in left prefrontal brain activity in the supplement group.

Among the foods that contain cognitive-beneficial carotenoids are foods with yellow, orange, or red fat-soluble plant pigments.

Foods High in Lutein and Zeaxanthin

- **Spinach**, raw, 1 cup: 3,659 micrograms (mcg)
- **Zucchini**, cooked, 1 cup: 2,070 mcg
- **Asparagus**, cooked, 1 cup: 1,388 mcg
- **Kale**, raw, 1 cup: 1,315 mcg
- **Corn**, yellow, frozen, 1 cup: 1,129 mcg
- **Carrots**, raw, 1 cup chopped: 328 mcg
- **Tomatoes**, canned, 1 cup: 321 mcg
- **Egg**, 1 large: 250 mcg

Source: USDA

Fish Oil Supplements

While eating fish is associated with a lower risk of cardiovascular disease, results of studies on the impact of taking fish oil supplements have been mixed. For example:

Heart disease

- **Pro:** A study published in 2021 found that taking supplements of EPA/DHA was linked with a lower risk of heart attack and other coronary heart disease events.

- **Con:** One large analysis found that fish oil supplements were not associated with a significantly reduced risk of death from coronary heart disease (CHD), or major vascular events such as stroke.

Brain health

- **Pro:** A study found that omega-3 supplements appear to be effective at improving EPA and DHA status, which may have a role in maintaining and supporting brain health, especially among people with low baseline levels, or for those with increased demands, such as breastfeeding mothers or people with diagnosed neuropsychiatric conditions.

- **Con:** A 2020 systematic review and meta-analysis of 38 randomized controlled trials with a total of 49,757 participants concluded that omega-3 fatty acid supplements do not protect older adults from cognitive decline. Since study participants' omega-3 levels at baseline are not known, however, it's possible the intervention didn't work because the participants in the analyzed studies were already high in omega-3s.

Beta-Carotene Supplement Cautions

Supplements of beta-carotene might have cognitive benefits, but evidence suggests these require being taken for an extended time. One study reported that men who took 50-milligram supplements of beta-carotene every other day for an average of 18 years did significantly better on cognitive tests, especially those measuring verbal memory, than those taking a placebo. The benefit was the mental equivalent of being one year younger. But no similar protection against brain aging was observed in individuals given the supplements for only a year.

Be aware, however, that smokers should not take extra beta-carotene because of an increased risk of lung cancer. Two well-designed clinical trials have reported that supplements of beta-carotene, alone or in combination with vitamin E supplements, increased the risk of lung cancer in smokers, compared to placebo.

Fish-Oil Pills

Should you be taking those popular fish-oil pills? The omega-3 fatty acids docosahexaenoic acid (DHA) and eicosapentaenoic acid (EPA) found in fish oil seem to help protect the brain. Logically, then, researchers have wondered: Could taking a fish-oil pill have similar benefits as eating fish? This theory has been more extensively studied than most hoped-for brain benefits from supplements, but to date the evidence is mixed, at best.

One of the largest and longest studies of its kind, a five-year clinical trial with more than 3,000 participants, reported no benefits from omega-3 supplements against cognitive decline. The study also found no significant benefits from supplements of lutein and zeaxanthin.

For this study, researchers took advantage of data from the Age-Related Eye Disease Study 2 (AREDS2), a follow-up to groundbreaking research that showed a combination of antioxidant vitamins could help slow the progression of age-related macular degeneration (AMD). AREDS2 tested the addition of DHA/EPA as well as lutein and zeaxanthin. Because many participants agreed to a battery of cognitive tests every two years, the data from the vision research also could be used to look for brain benefits—but none were found.

This otherwise definitive-seeming research may not be the final word, however. The study participants mostly came from a well-nourished, highly educated population, so it could be that supplementing their already healthy diet would not have much added benefit.

In another well-designed trial, Australian scientists tested fish-oil supplements versus an olive-oil placebo in 403 cognitively healthy volunteers, ages 65 to 90. Cognition was tested at the study's start and then every six months for 18 months. Compared to the control group, the fish-oil supplements did not maintain or improve cognitive performance and were associated with a small negative effect on psychomotor speed.

Jury Still Out

It's too soon, however, to close the book on hopes for brain benefits from fish-oil supplements. In another study, among healthy older adults not already suffering cognitive decline, large supplements of DHA (800 to 900 mg/day) improved verbal, visuospatial, and episodic memory. A lower dose of DHA—like that in most commercial fish-oil supplements—did not influence cognitive function, however.

In a study that used standard tests for memory and other mental abilities along with brain MRI scans, self-reported fish-oil supplementation was associated with significantly less brain atrophy and better scores on cognitive tests. No benefit was seen, however, among participants who already displayed mild cognitive impairments or Alzheimer's.

Nonetheless, a few studies showed benefits of omega-3s for individuals already suffering from cognitive impairment. One Chinese study investigated the effects of fish-oil supplements on older men and women diagnosed with mild cognitive impairment. After six months, supplementation was associated with improved test scores, better perceptual speed, space imagery efficiency, and working memory.

If you don't enjoy eating seafood or you're a vegan or vegetarian, it may be tempting to pop a pill instead of consuming salmon and other fatty fish. (Vegan EPA/DHA is obtained from algae.) But don't count on the pills to protect your brain—the evidence is still scant.

The B Vitamin Puzzle

Scientists have also studied B vitamins for possible brain benefits. Most research on B vitamins and cognition has focused on the role of homocysteine, an amino acid associated with cardiovascular disease. Homocysteine may be linked to stroke and vascular dementia, and some studies found high levels in the brains of people with Alzheimer's disease. Deficiencies of B_6, B_{12}, and folate are associated with higher homocysteine levels because they are necessary for metabolism of this amino acid; without adequate B vitamins, homocysteine builds up. So, it makes biological sense that taking supplemental B vitamins would benefit your brain (see "Too Much Thiamine Linked to Decline").

For example, a study of data on 2,420 older adults from national nutrition surveys reported that low vitamin B_{12} was associated with cognitive impairment both independently and in an interactive manner with high folate.

Similarly, a recent study reported that low blood levels of both vitamin B_{12} and folate are associated with poorer cognitive function. The 1,408 participants, average age 57, underwent a battery of cognitive tests and had blood drawn to test B vitamin levels. The study also reflected the puzzling complexity of B vitamins and cognition, as an imbalance of high folic acid and low vitamin B_{12} was associated with poorer function.

Deficiency and Dementia Risk

So, the takeaway may seem simple: Get your B vitamins. But the big picture is puzzling. It's true that the importance of B vitamins to brain function can easily be seen in the symptoms of deficiency, which include depression, cognitive decline, and dementia. Older people even just mildly deficient in B_{12} are at greater risk of cognitive decline. Vitamins B_6, B_{12}, and folate are essential to energy production, DNA/RNA repair, and neurotransmitter synthesis, including dopamine and serotonin.

Putting this theory to the test, however, proves not so simple. Taking B vitamin supplements, even when they succeed in lowering homocysteine levels, doesn't necessarily protect the brain. A Dutch study of almost 3,000 older adults with elevated levels of homocysteine randomly assigned participants to a placebo or a daily tablet containing 400 micrograms of folic acid and 500 micrograms of vitamin B_{12}. As expected, those given the supplements saw their homocysteine levels decline almost four times as much as those of the control group. But after two years, cognitive scores between the two groups differed only slightly.

Similarly, a meta-analysis pooled four clinical trials testing supplements of folic acid along with vitamin B_{12} and/or vitamin B_6. The intervention groups receiving extra B vitamins saw significantly lower homocysteine levels compared with the control groups. Again, however, cognitive testing failed to find any significant difference between the groups.

B Vitamin Takeaways

One possible explanation for these contrary results could be that supplemental B vitamins benefit only certain people, such as those initially with a low intake

NEW FINDING

Too Much Thiamine Linked to Decline

A study conducted in China revealed an intriguing pattern in the connection between dietary thiamine intake (vitamin B_1) and cognitive function in older adults. The research spanned nearly six years and involved tracking cognitive decline in relation to varying levels of thiamine consumption among 3,106 participants, average age 63. At a thiamine intake between 0.60 to 1.00 mg/day (slightly below the Recommended Dietary Allowance, or RDA), cognitive decline risk was minimal. However, beyond a certain threshold of 0.68 mg/day, a notable shift occurred: The relationship between thiamine intake and cognitive decline took on a J-shaped curve, indicating that too much thiamine might be detrimental to cognitive health. For each additional 1.0-mg increase in daily thiamine intake beyond the inflection point, there was a significant decline in global cognitive scores. This decline was particularly pronounced in individuals with obesity or hypertension and in nonsmokers. Thiamine, found in foods like whole grains, meat, and fish, is an essential nutrient for brain function. While previous studies have suggested a positive link between thiamine intake and cognitive health, this research underscores the importance of maintaining an optimal balance to support cognitive function in aging populations.

General Psychiatry, February 2024

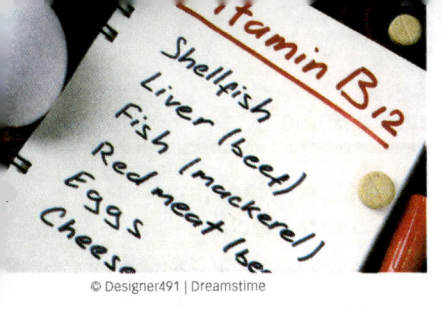

Older adults sometimes have difficulty obtaining enough vitamin B_{12} from foods, so discuss with your doctor if vitamin B_{12} is one supplement you should be using.

Sources of Vitamin B_{12}

These food servings provide at least 25 percent of the recommended dietary allowance of vitamin B_{12}:

- **Clams,** cooked, 3 oz.
- **Rainbow trout,** 3 oz.
- **Sockeye salmon,** 3 oz.
- **Lean top sirloin,** broiled, 3 oz.
- **Plain nonfat yogurt,** 1 cup
- **Fortified breakfast cereal,** 1 cup

Older people with lower levels of stomach acid, or who take acid-reducing medications for heartburn, may be at greater risk of deficiency. The form of the vitamin found in supplements and fortified foods does not require stomach acids to release it.

of B vitamins or elevated homocysteine levels. One study, dubbed VITACOG, compared the effects of high-dose B-complex supplements versus a placebo in older adults. Those given the extra B vitamins experienced slower brain atrophy. As in other studies, the benefits were greatest among subjects with elevated blood levels of homocysteine.

Last year, we learned of an analysis of data on almost 800 older adults given either extra folic acid or a placebo. At baseline and after three years, participants were given a battery of cognitive tests. All had elevated levels of homocysteine. Researchers also looked at participants' levels of omega-3 fatty acids, like those in fish oil. The treatment effect of the extra folic acid turned out to be significantly larger in participants low in omega-3s. Those at the highest omega-3 levels did not benefit from folic acid supplementation. Researchers concluded: "The results potentially explain the inconsistency in outcomes of B-vitamin supplementation trials and emphasize the importance of a personalized approach."

It could also be that homocysteine is simply a marker for cognitive impairment related to cerebrovascular disease, rather than a cause. Tufts scientists used MRI scans to find an association between the prevalence of small-vessel disease in the brain and difficulties with executive function. When these findings were compared with participants' homocysteine levels, scientists saw a relationship between homocysteine levels and cognitive impairment only when there were signs of this cerebrovascular pathology.

B_{12} for Older Adults

Another complication is that older adults sometimes have difficulty obtaining adequate amounts of vitamin B_{12} from food because of changes to the gastrointestinal system due to aging. Certain medications, such as stomach-acid blockers, also can contribute to the risk of B_{12} deficiency.

Dietary guidelines recommend that people ages 50 and older consume foods fortified with vitamin B_{12} and/or B_{12} supplements; both fortification and pills use a synthetic form of the vitamin that doesn't depend on stomach acids to release it.

While extra B vitamins might not have clear brain benefits, it's important to avoid deficiency. One study found that people with insufficient levels of B_{12} were at a greater risk of cognitive decline over nearly five years of follow-up than those with adequate levels of the vitamin. Very low levels of B_{12} also predicted decreased total brain volume.

Tufts scientists have found that even if you're only a little low in vitamin B_{12}, you might be at a greater risk for cognitive decline than previously thought. The study divided participants, average age 75, into five groups based on their blood levels of vitamin B_{12}. Scores on cognitive tests declined slightly overall, but average declines were significantly faster in both the lowest and second-lowest groups ranked by their vitamin B_{12} status.

The bottom line? You don't need to overdo B vitamins in hopes of turning back the clock on your brain. Make sure you're consuming adequate amounts from foods. Also consider adding fortified foods and supplements to your diet, if necessary, if you're over age 50.

Seeking Vitamin D Benefits

Vitamin D supplements, the subject of recent disappointing clinical trials, are back in the headlines with a flurry of promising results. In addition to the U.K. Biobank study detailed at the beginning of this chapter, an observational study reported an association between vitamin D exposure from supplements and sharply lower dementia risks. The study was published in *Alzheimer's & Dementia: Diagnosis, Assessment & Disease Monitoring* in January/March 2023.

Researchers looked at data on vitamin D supplementation and incident dementia in 12,388 initially dementia-free people from the National Alzheimer's Coordinating Center. Over 10 years, exposure to extra vitamin D at baseline was associated with a 40 percent lower subsequent dementia risk and longer dementia-free survival times. Associations were stronger among females and those without genetic risks for Alzheimer's. Scientists say, however, that data on vitamin D dosing and baseline levels were not available and that the observational study could not prove cause and effect.

Similarly, a Tufts study of nearly 1,100 seniors found that higher levels of vitamin D were associated with higher scores on tests of executive function, such as planning, organizing, and abstract thinking.

These encouraging results come with the ink barely dry on a two-year study of vitamin D supplementation and cognitive performance that found no benefit from extra doses. Researchers analyzed data from a clinical trial of 273 older adults (average age 70.3) whose primary goal was testing vitamin D supplements' effects on knee osteoarthritis. Because the participants were given an initial standard cognitive test, researchers were able to compare with follow-up mental testing. The trial tested 800 IU supplements of vitamin D against 2,000 IU pills. No differences were found in any cognitive measurements between the groups receiving 800 IU or 2,000 IU.

Deficiency Downsides

As science sorts this out, one thing is clear: Make sure you're getting enough of the "sunshine vitamin" from a combination of food, sun exposure (which makes vitamin D in the skin), and supplements if necessary.

In a review of the evidence on vitamin D and the brain, scientists reported that in 18 out of 25 cross-sectional observational studies, low vitamin D levels were linked to poorer scores on tests of cognitive functioning or higher frequency of dementia. And four out of six prospective observational studies showed a higher risk of cognitive decline after a follow-up period of four to seven years in participants with initial lower vitamin D levels.

A large study found that older individuals deficient in vitamin D were significantly more likely to develop dementia and Alzheimer's over almost six years of follow-up than individuals with higher blood levels of the vitamin (see "Low Vitamin D Linked to Alzheimer's Risk").

Getting Your D. Adults need 15 micrograms (600 IU) daily of vitamin D; that recommendation rises to 20 micrograms (800 IU) after age 70. The ability of your skin to produce vitamin D declines with age, and older people often spend less time in the sun. People who live in northern regions have difficulty making enough vitamin D in the winter because the Earth's position limits the strength of the ultraviolet B rays.

Vitamin D is present in some foods, but it can be difficult to get adequate amounts from dietary sources alone. Natural sources of vitamin D include some types of fish, whole eggs, and some mushrooms. Some foods and beverages, including many brands of milk and plant milks, orange juice, and breakfast cereals, are fortified with vitamin D.

Vitamin E and Alzheimer's

Some research suggests that another nutrient important for overall health—vitamin E—could also help protect your brain. A study of more than 600 mostly male patients at veteran's hospitals compared a placebo with three treatments for those with mild or moderate Alzheimer's: high-dose (2,000 IU daily) vitamin E supplements; a combination of vitamin E and memantine (Namenda), a drug shown to have modest benefits in moderate-to-severe Alzheimer's; and memantine alone. Only the vitamin E

Vitamin D Food Sources

Adults under 70 years old need a daily intake of at least 600 IU (international units) of vitamin D per day. Those 70 and over need 800 IU per day.

FOOD	VITAMIN D INTERNATIONAL UNITS (IU)
Trout, farmed, 3 oz	645
Salmon (sockeye) 3 oz	570
Mushrooms*, ½ cup	366
Milk, fortified, 1 cup	120
Soymilk, fortified, 1 cup	120
Sardines, canned, 2	46
Egg yolk, 1 large	44
Beef liver, 3 oz	42
Tuna, canned, 3 oz	40

*Mushrooms must be exposed to natural sunlight or artificial UV light to contain vitamin D.

NEW FINDING

Low Vitamin D Linked to Alzheimer's Risk

Previous studies have linked low blood levels of vitamin D to greater risk of dementia, but these findings have varied when it comes to associations specifically with Alzheimer's disease. So, scientists set out to conduct a review of the evidence, pooling five prospective trials and one cross-sectional study. The meta-analysis concluded that individuals with low vitamin D serum levels (below 25 ng/ml) had a 59 percent increased risk of developing Alzheimer's disease compared with patients with normal vitamin D levels. Scientists cautioned, however, that "Further research is required to provide evidence on whether maintaining sufficient vitamin D serum levels may lower the risk of Alzheimer's disease."

Egyptian Journal of Neurology, Psychiatry and Neurosurgery, July 3, 2013

Getting vitamin E from food is considered far less risky than using supplements, which may have negative effects.

NEW FINDING

Brain Protection from Multivitamins

Studies of cognitive benefits from multivitamins have produced mixed results over the years. Now, however, a meta-analysis of three separate studies of taking a daily multivitamin "provides strong and consistent evidence" that the supplements help prevent memory loss and slow cognitive aging, according to researchers. They estimated that the daily multivitamin slowed global cognitive aging by the equivalent of two years compared with a placebo. The study was the third to report cognitive benefits from multivitamins using data from the COcoa Supplement and Multivitamin Outcomes Study (COSMOS), which originally aimed to test cocoa extract and multivitamins for cardiovascular and cancer protection. Of the more than 21,000 COSMOS participants, ages 60 and older, some 5,200 also completed cognitive tests. Among that group, in three sub-studies, daily multivitamin supplementation showed a benefit in global cognition and episodic memory, compared with a placebo.

American Journal of Clinical Nutrition, Jan. 18, 2024

group (without the drug) saw any benefit, a small but statistically significant improvement in performance on tests of functional impairment over a period of more than two years. All three groups declined in their ability to perform tasks of daily living.

The results, experts cautioned, are specific to individuals already suffering with moderate-to-severe Alzheimer's disease and can't be generalized to a healthy population. Other trials of vitamin E supplementation have failed to find a link between vitamin E supplements and the risk of cognitive decline.

In addition, two clinical trials showed an increased risk of hemorrhagic stroke in participants taking vitamin E. And results from the SELECT trial showed that vitamin E supplements may harm adult men in the general population by increasing their risk of prostate cancer.

News on Multivitamins

If you're like many Americans, you probably take a multivitamin/mineral supplement. Multivitamins account for 40 percent of sales of vitamin and mineral supplements—at a cost of nearly $6 billion annually. An estimated one-third of all U.S. adults regularly take multivitamin/mineral supplements. Many Americans view multivitamin pills as insurance against nutritional shortfalls from their diets—a notion that is controversial among nutrition experts.

Can taking a pill containing nutrients believed to be beneficial for your brain, such as those found in a multivitamin, have the same effects as eating healthy foods? The results are isappointing results. For reasons scientists can't fully explain, vitamins and minerals consumed in whole foods seem to affect the body differently than when popped in pill form. It may be that synergistic relationships between nutrients trigger benefits that are not present in isolation.

For example, in the Physicians' Health Study II, 5,947 men, average age 71.6, were randomly assigned to receive either a daily multivitamin or a placebo. The analysis combined five tests of global cognitive function and testing verbal memory. Over an average follow-up of 8.5 years, changes in mental function were no different in the multivitamin group than in those taking a placebo. Researchers concluded, "These data do not provide support for use of multivitamin supplements in the prevention of cognitive decline."

In the past year or so, however, the COSMOS trial has offered a glimmer of hope for cognitive benefits from multivitamins. A meta-analysis of three separate studies of taking a daily multivitamin "provides strong and consistent evidence" that the supplements help prevent memory loss and slow cognitive aging, according to researchers (see "Brain Protection from Multivitamins").

Bottom line here: If you're already taking a daily multivitamin, there's no reason to stop, and there might be evidence of some cognitive benefit.

Nutrient Essentials

These studies may help explain why some dietary patterns and some specific foods may offer cognitive protection. But the results of research on these same nutrients in pill form are decidedly mixed, emphasizing the importance of dietary choices over drugstore shortcuts.

With advice from your health-care professional, you might decide to supplement your dietary intake of vitamin B_{12} and/or vitamin D, which you could be falling short on as you age. Most people get plenty of the other vitamins and minerals found in multivitamins simply by consuming a variety of healthy foods.

No matter which way you turn it, the strongest benefit nutritionally comes from food, not a bottle.

8 The Facts on "Brain Boost" Pills

Even though much of the science behind the connections between diet and heart-brain health remains unsettled, the research is voluminous, painstaking, and independent.

For example, the government's PubMed database contains more than 8,000 studies of the possible effects of omega-3 supplementation. The fact that some of these pills' benefits continue to be elusive only demonstrates the high evidence standards that nutrition scientists demand.

It might surprise you, then, to learn that the research supporting many of the best-selling "brain power," "brain energy," "memory," and "mental focus" supplements falls far short of these standards. Indeed, the most popular memory supplement has been studied only a handful of times in a small clinical trial conducted by scientists employed by the manufacturer. Those results were not published in any influential or highly regarded peer-reviewed journal.

When such brain health supplements have been more widely studied by independent scientists, as with gingko biloba, the results have mostly been disappointing. There's reason to be equally skeptical of products marketed as "brain vitamins" or "vitamins for memory" or that promise a "strong brain."

None of this is to say that there's no potential for supplements to improve memory or protect the aging brain. But the evidence for these products falls far short of the research we've been exploring in the previous chapters. It's not really accurate to say the jury is still out on most brain-boosting pills; rather, the jury has not even been empaneled yet.

"A Huge Waste of Money"

This paucity of evidence notwithstanding, more than 25 percent of Americans ages 50 to 73 and 36 percent of those age 74 and up take supplements for brain health, seeking to improve memory. This popularity, fueled by online hype and

Healthy Heart, Healthy Brain | 51

NEW FINDING

Memory Supplements Evidence Mixed

A new review of the evidence finds a mixed bag for efficacy in the $7.6 billion U.S. brain health supplement industry. Scientists looked at research on more than 100 products found in national pharmacies and groceries to identify the 18 most common brain-supplement ingredients. The review found no compelling evidence for use of apoaequorin (Prevagen), coenzyme Q_{10}, coffee extracts, L-theanine, omega-3 fatty acids, vitamin B_6, vitamin B_9, or vitamin B_{12} supplementation for memory. On the other hand, some current evidence supports memory benefits from supplementation with ashwagandha, choline, curcumin, ginger, lion's mane, polyphenols, phosphatidylserine, and turmeric. There are current studies with mixed results regarding the benefit of carnitine, gingko biloba, Huperzine A, vitamin D, and vitamin E supplementation for memory. Reviewers concluded: "Dietary supplements geared toward improving cognition are a billion-dollar industry that continues to grow despite lacking a solid scientific foundation for their marketing claims. More rigorous studies are needed relative to the long-term use of these supplements in homogenous populations with standardized measurements of cognition."

CNS Drugs, September 2023

---

relentless television commercials, comes despite a report from the AARP-founded Global Council on Brain Health (GCBH) that concluded most supplements to preserve or boost memory or cognition aren't worth the plastic they're bottled in (see "Memory Supplements Evidence Mixed"). The panel of top neurologists, nutritionists, and researchers concluded, "Supplements for brain health appear to be a huge waste of money for the 25 percent of adults over 50 who take them."

An AARP analysis of spending on just six different supplements marketed for brain health shows that adults ages 50 and older spend more than $93 million a month on these proprietary blends alone. "These people taking these pills are spending between $20 and $60 a month and flushing dollars down the toilet that could be better spent on things that improve their brain health," the GCBH reported.

The AARP also warned that some people should be especially cautious about taking these supplements because of possible health risks and drug interactions.

Understanding Supplements

It's worth keeping in mind that supplements claiming to improve memory and stave off age-related cognitive decline aren't truly supplements. That is, although some toss in B vitamins and other nutrients, their main ingredients don't *supplement* any biological need. There's no Recommended Daily Allowance (RDA) for ginkgo biloba, for example.

The reason these dubious products are referred to as "supplements" goes back to a quirk in federal regulation. While the U.S. Food & Drug Administration (FDA) has the power to ensure the safety of medications and foods and regulate health claims, "dietary supplements" fall under the 1994 Dietary Supplement Health and Education Act (DSHEA). Supplement makers' products—unlike prescription drugs—are not regulated by the FDA for effectiveness before they are permitted to be sold. Under DSHEA, the manufacturer is responsible for the accuracy and truthfulness of product claims. These statements must be submitted to the FDA within 30 days of use but are not verified by the U.S. government.

You've probably seen the familiar fine-print disclaimer on product labels and ads complying with DSHEA: "This statement has not been evaluated by the FDA. This product is not intended to diagnose, treat, cure, or prevent any disease." Nonetheless, manufacturers can make carefully crafted promises—"structure-function claims" permitted under DSHEA—that their products, for example, "enhance mental sharpness and support long-term brain health." They cannot say the product will "prevent Alzheimer's disease," however. Another government agency, the Federal Trade Commission (FTC), can step in only when it detects false advertising.

Unregulated, Unknown Ingredients

These regulatory loopholes also mean that when you buy supplements, you have few guarantees of their purity, or even whether the products contain the ingredients listed on the label. One study using DNA testing found that four out of five popular herbal remedies sold at leading retailers didn't contain *any* of the promised ingredients—just fillers, some of which could pose risks for people with intolerances or allergies. For example, pills sold as ginkgo biloba, a Chinese tree touted for memory benefits (see next page), contained powdered radish, ground houseplants, and wheat.

In another study, scientists reported that one-third of 44 herbal remedies tested contained no trace of the supposed main ingredient at all. And nearly 60 percent of the products contained DNA from at least one plant species that wasn't listed on the product label. Some

St. John's wort, for instance, contained senna, which can be toxic if taken regularly and can cause chronic diarrhea and damage the colon and the liver.

To be safe, stick to products that have been tested and verified by independent organizations.

Ginkgo Biloba

A common ingredient in "brain-boosting" and "focus" supplements is a traditional Chinese herbal remedy derived from the leaves of the ginkgo tree, ginkgo biloba, which can also be bought on its own. Although ginkgo biloba is the most-studied such supplement ingredient, results have been mixed at best. A report from the government's National Center for Complementary and Integrative Health (NCCIH) concluded: "There's no conclusive evidence that ginkgo biloba is efficacious in preventing or slowing dementia or cognitive decline."

A few small, early studies suggested ginkgo biloba may slightly improve some symptoms of dementia, but newer studies have shown no effect. The largest clinical trial ever conducted on the effect of ginkgo supplements on dementia prevention was the Ginkgo Evaluation of Memory Study (GEM), published in 2008. This eight-year randomized controlled trial gave 240 milligrams (mg) a day of ginkgo biloba extract or placebo to more than 3,000 older adults with normal cognitive function or mild cognitive impairment at baseline. There was no significant difference in risk of dementia or Alzheimer's disease (or progression to dementia if they had mild cognitive impairment) between participants receiving the supplement and those in the placebo group.

Subsequently, GEM also found that twice-daily doses of 120 mg of ginkgo biloba extract worked no better than a placebo in slowing cognitive decline.

Since then, a review of 21 trials with 2,608 total participants did find some positives for the traditional remedy. Compared with conventional medicine alone, ginkgo biloba in combination with conventional medicine was superior in improving Mini-Mental State Examination (MMSE) scores at 24 weeks for patients with Alzheimer's disease or mild cognitive impairment. The addition of ginkgo biloba also was associated with better scores on activity of daily living tests among patients with Alzheimer's.

Consuming moderate amounts (120 to 240 mg) of ginkgo biloba appears to be safe for most people. Possible side effects include headache, stomach upset, dizziness, palpitations, constipation, and allergic skin reactions. Ginkgo may interact with anticoagulant medications (blood thinners).

Should you give it a try? There's no conclusive evidence that Ginkgo is helpful for preserving or improving your cognitive health.

Green-Tea Powder

We've already seen that drinking green tea might have benefits for brain power, but what about green-tea powder, sold as a supplement? An analysis of nine interventional trials comparing green tea powder supplements to placebo found no significant effects on cognitive dysfunction. Other trials providing individual tea components (like catechins and L-theanine) have noted some improvement in specific areas of cognition, but these individual studies have been small and need to be confirmed in larger studies.

In addition to possible cognitive benefits, green tea may combat depression. In one Japanese study, elderly participants who reported drinking four or more cups of green tea per day were 44 percent less likely to have symptoms of depression than those drinking one cup or less per day. A similar relationship was seen for green tea consumption and risk of severe depression. It's not clear whether similar benefits might be associated with green tea powder, however.

© Goory | Dreamstime

Consuming small amounts of ginkgo biloba, which is made from the leaves of the ginkgo biloba tree, appears safe for most people and may help combat cognitive decline.

Confusing Claims

Look out for claims on brain supplements that seem to promise health benefits while skirting the letter of the law on FDA regulations. You might think that these products can help prevent Alzheimer's, dementia, or cognitive decline, but the FDA doesn't permit such direct claims without proof, which the products don't have. Instead, ads and labels use language like this:

- "healthy brain function and memory improvement"
- "clinically shown to safely and effectively improve memory"
- "helps support memory and learning"
- "shown to increase levels of BDNF, a vital neuroprotein for brain health"
- "improve memory, concentration, and focus"
- "improves recall and short-term memory"

Healthy Heart, Healthy Brain | 53

Curcumin Smarts

- Understand that the potential health benefits of turmeric/curcumin remain unproven.
- Choose curcumin, not turmeric. A study found that turmeric powders contiain only about 3 percent curcumin.
- Tell your doctor before starting curcumin (or any) supplements. Curcumin can interact with medications, including anticoagulants.
- Check ingredients. If you do choose to take curcumin supplements, make sure they contain piperine or other ingredients proven to boost absorption.
- Take with food. Taken on an empty stomach, curcumin supplements may cause gastritis and peptic ulcer disease. Additionally, curcumin is fat-soluble, so it will be better absorbed in the presence of fat (stick with plant fats over animal fats).
- Discontinue use if you note any adverse reactions, such as nausea, diarrhea, or headaches.
- Don't take if pregnant or lactating. The safety of curcumin supplements in pregnancy and lactation has not been established.

Green tree extract appears to be safe at levels around 1.6 grams a day. The maximum tolerated dose in humans is reported to be 9.9 grams per day. There is some evidence for liver toxicity at high doses.

Randomized controlled trials have found green tea powder supplements have no significant effect on cognitive health. There is some interesting emerging science on some tea components, but more research is needed.

Ginseng and Grape Seed Extract

You may also see products containing ginseng or grape seed extract, or these plant products by themselves, marketed for brain benefits (and other claims). An NCCIH review concluded there's not enough evidence to recommend either for protection against dementia and Alzheimer's disease.

Grape seed extract contains an antioxidant compound, oligomeric proanthocyanidin (OPC), which has been studied for a variety of health conditions. A few preliminary studies have looked at possible effects on the brain, but the NCCIH says, "There is currently insufficient evidence to determine if grape seed extract is helpful in the prevention or treatment of cognitive decline or Alzheimer's disease."

Exercise caution with grape seed extract if you have a bleeding disorder, are going to have surgery, or you take anticoagulants (blood thinners), such as warfarin or aspirin.

Turmeric/Curcumin

Another naturally occurring compound that's being studied for possible brain benefits is turmeric, the golden-orange spice known for imparting a yellow hue to curries and mustards. This plant rhizome, which resembles ginger root, has been used in traditional medicine for centuries. One clue that turmeric might be protective for cognition was the finding that people living in countries in which curry is a staple of the diet have much lower rates of Alzheimer's disease than people in the United States.

Today, curcumin, a polyphenol compound partly responsible for turmeric's color, is getting a lot of attention from researchers for potential health benefits, including possible brain benefits.

Curcumin shows antioxidant and anti-inflammatory properties in cultured cells, and animal studies have been promising, but human studies have been less certain. One review that analyzed eight randomized controlled trials totaling 389 participants (a modest number) found some improvement in working memory and a possible improvement in brain processing speed in the curcumin group versus the placebo group. There were no significant changes in multiple other cognitive domains. Participants in the curcumin group had a significantly higher risk of side effects, such as gastrointestinal upset and diarrhea, than those in the placebo group.

It's possible that curcumin could be effective in countering depression and improving mood, because it seems to increase levels of the mood-enhancing neurotransmitters serotonin and dopamine. Much like the antidepressants called monoamine oxidase (MAO) inhibitors, curcumin blocks the enzymes responsible for breaking down serotonin and dopamine. Animal tests have shown that curcumin enhances the antidepressant effects of medications, such as fluoxetine (Prozac) and venlafaxine (Effexor).

Even though evidence for curcumin's benefits remains preliminary, turmeric now can be found not only in supermarket spice aisles but also in stores selling vitamins and other supplements. In supplement form, it may be labeled as turmeric or curcumin or both.

Clinical trials mostly have not been able to demonstrate the hoped-for benefits, a disappointment broadly attributed to difficulties with absorption, bioavailability, and the timing and length of intervention. Dietary intake is not sufficient to provide the levels of curcumin being studied for therapeutic benefits. To reach those levels, dietary supplements would be necessary. For example, 1,500 mg of curcumin—an amount used in some studies—is equivalent to about 7.5 teaspoons of turmeric.

Studies support the safety of 6 grams a day of oral curcumin supplements for four to seven weeks. Some people experience stomach upset, nausea, dizziness, or diarrhea, especially at higher doses. People on anticoagulant drugs (blood thinners) and diabetes medications should not take turmeric or curcumin supplements without consulting their healthcare provider. Independent testing found supplements did not always contain the expected level of active compounds.

Creatine for Mental Muscles

Unless you're an athlete or bodybuilder, you might not be familiar with creatine supplements, which total sales of over $400 million a year but are not typically viewed as a "brain booster." Creatine is used to increase muscle mass and improve performance in intense physical competitions, such as cycling or rowing. You can obtain creatine naturally in the diet through the consumption of high-protein foods, such as meat, fish, and eggs. The body also synthesizes creatine from amino acids.

Creatine is found in the brain as well as the muscles, leading to speculation that extra creatine might strengthen mental "muscles." One review of the evidence concluded: "In relation to the brain, creatine has been shown to have antioxidant properties, reduce mental fatigue, protect the brain from neurotoxicity, and improve facets/components of neurological disorders like depression and bipolar disorder."

Patients with Alzheimer's disease have decreased activity of a creatine enzyme in key areas of the brain, compared with healthy people of the same age. It's possible that differences in this creatine enzyme contribute to the abnormal metabolism and neuron loss and dysfunction seen in Alzheimer's patients. Creatine also prevents oxidative damage, suggesting it might protect against beta-amyloid-induced oxidative stress in patients with Alzheimer's disease.

Studying Creatine

In animal testing, mice and rats fed a diet enhanced with creatine displayed improved memory and learning ability. In studies of healthy humans, supplemental creatine significantly improved working memory and intelligence scores among vegetarians and vegans, who are likely to have low creatine intake from their diets.

Supplements of creatine helped relieve mental fatigue after an exam and improved the mental performance of young men suffering from sleep deprivation. In a test of healthy non-vegetarians not subjected to any unusual stress, however, creatine supplementation did not improve cognitive scores.

Nonetheless, people suffering from age-related cognitive decline might benefit. One study found creatine improved performance on tests of verbal and spatial short- and long-term memory.

According to the National Library of Medicine, creatine is likely safe when taken by mouth at doses up to 25 grams daily for up to 14 days. Lower doses, up to 4 to 5 grams taken daily for up to 18 months, also are likely safe.

Side effects can include stomach pain, nausea, diarrhea, and muscle cramping. Creatine causes muscles to draw water from the rest of your body, so you will need to drink extra water to avoid dehydration. People with bipolar disorder or kidney disease (or conditions such as diabetes that increase the risk of kidney disease) should not use creatine supplements.

Creatine is often recommended for bodybuilders to increase muscle mass and is now found to help reduce mental fatigue.

NEW FINDING

Neuriva Shows Promise

"Brain boosting" supplements are rarely subjected to the "gold standard" of scientific research, so a randomized, double-blind, placebo-controlled study of Neuriva is worth noting. The study examined the effects of 42 days of supplementation with the coffee-cherry extract and phosphatidylserine pills on memory, accuracy, focus, and concentration and learning among 138 healthy adults (ages 40 to 65) with self-reported memory problems. Standardized testing found improvements in the supplement group, compared with placebo, in memory, accuracy, focus and concentration, and reaction time. Three other tests, including levels of the BDNF compound phosphatidylserine is thought to improve, showed no difference.

Neurology and Therapy, June 2023

Nootropics

The term "nootropics" might be new to you, but you've probably heard of some of these "smart drug" products—and maybe even tried them. What's in them? Some nootropic manufacturers boast about the sources of their key ingredients, while others disclose only the bare minimum. Either way, you should approach these products with a skeptical eye. Here's what we know about the ingredients in some of the most popular brain supplements:

Apoaequorin. This protein "originally found in jellyfish" is the key ingredient in the most widely advertised nootropic, Prevagen. This protein is claimed to help protect your memory—even though jellyfish don't have brains. Then there's the matter of the blood-brain barrier, which jellyfish proteins are unlikely to cross, as well as what happens to proteins in your stomach. Even the manufacturer's own safety studies show that apoaequorin is rapidly digested in the stomach and broken down into amino acids and small peptides like any other dietary protein.

The only study of apoaequorin's effectiveness (as opposed to safety) cited on Prevagen's website was conducted by an employee and was not published in a peer-reviewed journal. Most recently, a 2020 study reported short-term memory improvements in aged rats.

Given the cost of Prevagen—more than $1 a day and about $3 a day for "professional strength"—independent experts advise there are more-proven investments in your brain power, like a healthy diet and a gym membership.

Coffee Fruit Extract. This is one of the two main ingredients in the original formulation of Neuriva, a dietary brain supplement. Made from the plant waste left over after coffee beans have been processed, this extract has been shown in a handful of studies to increase brain-derived neurotrophic factor (BDNF). BDNF stimulates the production of new brain cells; it also protects brain cells from damage and stimulates their connections. Evidence that increasing BDNF levels benefits cognition is limited, however. In some studies, rats with boosted BDNF did better navigating mazes; in others, they didn't (see "Neuriva Shows Promise").

An article in *Psychology Today* reviewed the evidence and called it "Neuriva nonsense" and "just another snake oil." A 2023 clinical trial, however, did report benefits among people with self-reported memory problems, compared with a placebo.

Phosphatidylserine (PS). The other key ingredient in Neuriva, this fat-like substance is found naturally in cell membranes, especially in the brain. PS is extracted from soybeans and often sold in combination with other memory boosters. Promoters boast that PS is the only such ingredient with a qualified health claim approved by the FDA. They are less likely to note the FDA's qualification that "there is little scientific evidence for this claim." Nonetheless, it's true that a few small, short-term studies have shown promising results with PS in elderly subjects already suffering from memory problems.

According to the review in *Psychology Today*, however, "Thirty years ago, neuroscientists were excited about phosphatidylserine's potential—but not anymore. Essentially, dietary supplements cannot increase phosphatidylserine levels in the brain. Those older studies suggested some slight cognitive improvements for elderly people, but these cognitive changes were never considered clinically relevant, and phosphatidylserine is no longer considered worthwhile."

Huperzine A. This moss extract, originally a Chinese herbal remedy, is thought to increase brain levels of the neurotransmitter acetylcholine. One review of the evidence in 10 trials in patients with Alzheimer's disease or vascular dementia concluded that Huperzine A could "significantly improve" cognitive scores. Those findings, however, do not mean that Huperzine A protects against cognitive decline in healthy individuals, as is claimed by manufacturers of some supplement formulations. Another positive review cautioned about the findings "due to the poor methodological quality of the included trials."

Bacopa Monnieri. A traditional herb used in Ayurvedic medicine, bacopa monnieri has been studied for memory, spatial learning, and nerve-cell benefits. Despite some positive findings, most of the research done with this herb is almost a decade old, and evidence for its effectiveness remains limited. A 2022 review of five "very low certainty evidence" studies concluded there was no difference between bacopa monnieri and a placebo in the treatment of Alzheimer's disease.

Vinpocetine. This synthetic compound is made to resemble a substance found naturally in the periwinkle plant. It has been used in Europe to protect against strokes because it's thought to increase blood flow to the brain. By extension, vinpocetine also is hypothesized to improve brain function. Recent studies have focused on countering brain injuries and Parkinson's disease in animal testing.

Studies of vinpocetine's effectiveness on healthy humans are few and small. In studies of older adults with memory problems associated with poor brain circulation or dementia-related disease, however, vinpocetine produced significantly more improvement than a placebo on tests of attention, concentration, and memory.

Mood Supplements

Some brain supplements may also promise to boost mood, counter depression, improve sleep quality, and increase energy. The evidence for their effectiveness is mixed, though some may be safe alternatives to prescription medications.

Melatonin

A hormone that your brain produces in response to darkness, melatonin helps with the timing of your circadian rhythms and with sleep. According to the NCCIH, research suggests that melatonin plays other important roles in the body beyond sleep. However, these effects are not fully understood.

Melatonin supplements may help with certain conditions, such as jet lag, delayed sleep-wake phase disorder, some sleep disorders in children, and anxiety before and after surgery. Expert guidelines state that there's not enough strong evidence on effectiveness or safety to recommend melatonin supplementation for chronic insomnia.

N-acetylcysteine (NAC)

NAC is a supplement form of cysteine, an amino acid used by the body in the production of glutathione, an antioxidant made in the liver. Low levels of glutathione have been associated with mental health conditions, including depression. The body can produce cysteine from other amino acids found in protein-rich foods like chicken, yogurt, seeds, and legumes.

A 2022 review of the evidence for NAC found "the most evidence of having a beneficial effect as an adjuvant agent in the negative symptoms of schizophrenia, severe autism, depression, obsessive compulsive disorder, and related disorders." Scientists cautioned, however, that "most studies have been underpowered and perhaps too brief, with some evidence of benefit only after months of treatment with NAC."

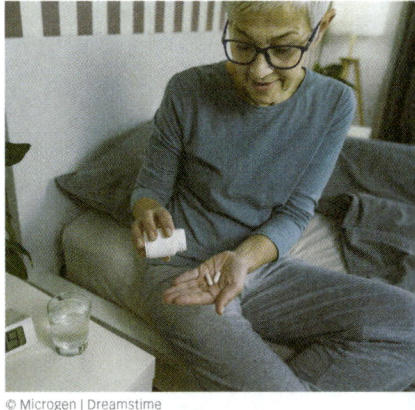

Melatonin may help with things like jet lag, but it may not be the bests choice for chronic insomnia.

St. John's wort is a pretty yellow flower that may or may not help with depression. One thing is clear, though: It can interfere with your medication, so consult your doctor before using it.

Go Verified

How can you be sure supplements contain what they say they do? Look for products with the "USP Verified" seal of the United States Pharmacopeia, an independent, nonprofit organization. Only products that have been voluntarily submitted to the USP and passed its testing can display the official seal (tinyurl.com/yr5w3xj8). (Don't be fooled by labels that simply use the letters "USP," suggesting that the manufacturer claims to follow the organization's standards but doesn't submit products for testing.) Only a few nationwide brands participate in the USP testing program, most notably NatureMade, TruNature, Kirkland (Costco), and Member's Mark (Sam's Club).

Another nonprofit, NSF International (nsf.org), focuses on products for athletes but also certifies some products such as multivitamins and fish oil. Two for-profit groups that test, rank, and review supplements are ConsumerLab (consumerlab.com) and LabDoor (labdoor.com).

SAMe

S-adenosylmethionine (SAMe) is made naturally in the body. A 2024 review found that SAMe "may provide relief of depression symptoms similar to imipramine or escitalopram" (prescription antidepressants). Reviewers urged caution, however, "due to the small number of studies and the large range of SAMe doses that were used in the included trials." SAMe may interact with some medicines and other dietary supplements, and it may not be safe for those with bipolar disorder and those who are immunocompromised. Recent studies have sought to understand the mechanism by which SAMe might alleviate depression. Other findings suggest a potential effect on cognitive impairment in brain aging, related to countering oxidative stress and inflammation.

St. John's Wort

St. John's wort is derived from a flowering plant traditionally harvested on St. John's Day (June 24). As a supplement, St. John's wort is an option for short-term treatment of mild depression, according to clinical guidelines from the American College of Physicians-American Society of Internal Medicine.

A review of the evidence about St. John's wort and major depression, published in the Cochrane Database, concluded that it was as effective as standard prescription antidepressants, with fewer side effects. The National Library of Medicine, however, cautions that, although some studies have reported benefits for depression, others have not. One large study sponsored by NCCIH found that St. John's wort was no more effective than a placebo in treating major depression of moderate severity.

Keep in mind that St. John's wort weakens the effects of a long list of medications, including the common blood thinner warfarin, so consult your physician before trying it. Taking St. John's wort with certain antidepressants or other drugs that affect the neurotransmitter serotonin may lead to potentially serious side effects. St. John's wort was among the herbal products found to frequently fail to contain the listed ingredient, so make sure you choose a brand that's been independently verified.

Valerian

This herbal remedy from the root of valerian, a flowering plant, has been used since ancient times. It may be effective against insomnia, although the NCCIH advises, "There is not enough evidence from well-designed studies to confirm this." Moreover, "There is not enough scientific evidence to determine whether valerian works for other conditions, such as anxiety or depression."

Valerian does not relieve insomnia as fast as standard sleep medications, and continuous use for several days, even up to four weeks, may be needed before an effect is noticeable. Some studies found that valerian doesn't improve insomnia any better than a placebo. Few side effects have been reported, but valerian should not be taken with alcohol or sedative medications.

Buyer Beware

If you've been inundated by TV commercials for "brain-boosting" supplements, you may have been surprised how dubious the claims are for most such products. The evidence that popping any pill can protect your brain power is thin.

As we'll see in the next chapter, exercise and other lifestyle changes may be the most promising way of all to protect your aging brain.

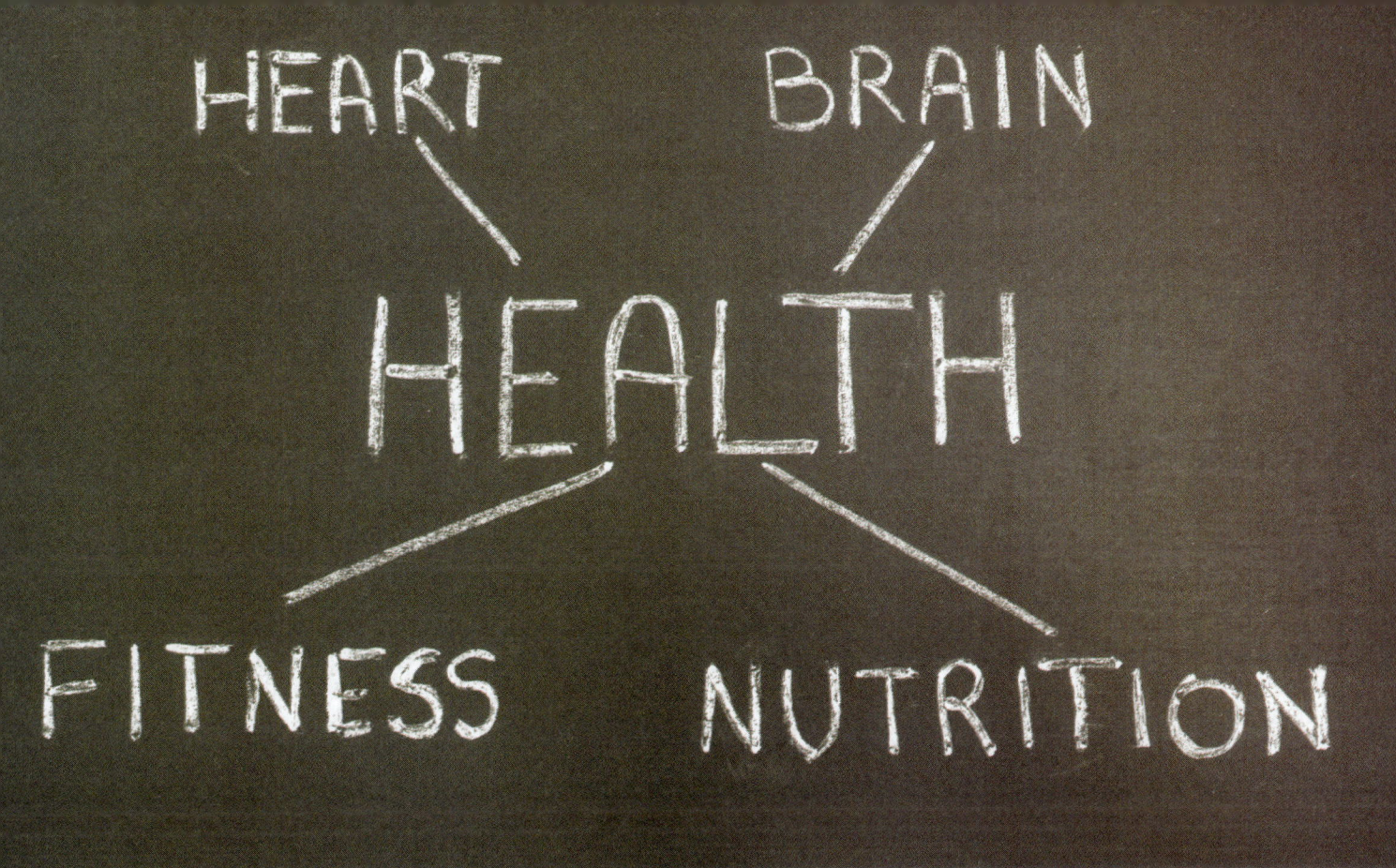

9 Heart-Brain Lifestyle Secrets

As much as a healthy diet can contribute to protecting your heart and brain, other smart lifestyle choices might be even more beneficial. Consider some of the findings we learned about last year:

Being physically active at any time in adulthood, and to any extent, is linked with higher later-life cognition, according to a study in the May 2023 *Journal of Neurology, Neurosurgery, and Psychiatry*. Researchers studied 1,417 Britons whose participation in leisure-time activity was recorded five times between the ages of 36 and 69. A battery of tests measured cognition at age 69, and scores were compared to prior activity levels. Being physically active, at all assessments in adulthood, was associated with higher cognition at age 69. The strongest association was between sustained cumulative physical activity and later-life cognition; as activity went up, so did cognitive performance. Those with the highest average cognition at 69 were participants categorized as moderately active (participated one to four times/month) and most active (participated five or more times per month).

Getting at least 3,800 steps per day might shave 25 percent off your risk of developing dementia—and increasing your step count further lowers risk, up to 9,800 steps daily. Those findings come from wrist-worn accelerometers tracking the

Common sense tells you it's important to take care of your heart and brain, but now you also know what lifestyle choices help you do that. In this chapter, we share more of what research is finding.

Stimulating Your Brain

Makers of products ranging from common crossword puzzles to online "brain challenge" games tout the benefits of mental as well as physical activity. Stimulating your brain does seem to offer cognitive protection—but you don't need pricey products to benefit. Researchers found that a "cognitively active" lifestyle in old age may delay the onset of dementia in Alzheimer's disease by as much as five years. The most effective activities emphasize seeking or processing information: time spent visiting a library, reading newspapers, reading magazines, reading books, writing letters, or playing games like puzzles, cards, and board games.

Classifying Aerobic Activity

Physical activity experts recommend adults aim for 150 minutes a week of moderate-intensity physical activity or 75 minutes a week of vigorous-intensity activity (plus strength training). The lists below give a general idea of what is commonly considered moderate- and vigorous-intensity activity.

MODERATE INTENSITY
- Ballroom dancing
- Baseball or softball
- Bicycling (<10 mph)
- Bowling
- Fishing and hunting
- Golf (without cart)
- Kayaking
- Mopping/vacuuming
- Shooting baskets
- Tai chi, yoga
- Walking briskly on a level surface
- Water aerobics
- Tennis (doubles)

VIGOROUS INTENSITY
- Aerobic dancing/step aerobics
- Backpacking
- Bicycling (>10 mph)
- Circuit or interval training
- Cross-country skiing
- Ice skating
- Jogging, running, or race walking
- Jumping rope
- Karate/kick boxing
- Rowing
- Soccer
- Swimming laps
- Tennis (singles)

---

steps of 78,430 participants in the U.K. Biobank, ages 40 to 79, published in *JAMA Neurology*, Sept. 6, 2022. Over an average follow-up of almost seven years, 866 participants developed dementia. Those reaching 9,800 steps daily were only half as likely to develop dementia as the most sedentary participants; those walking even more saw no additional benefit. Step intensity also mattered in reducing dementia risk, with the optimal pace at 112 steps per minute—characterized by researchers as "a rather brisk cadence."

Physical as well as mental activities, such as household chores, exercise, and visiting with family and friends, may help lower the risk of dementia, according to a study of more than a half-million people published in *Neurology*, Aug. 23, 2022. Participants (average age 56) were initially free of dementia. They were followed an average of 11 years, during which 5,185 developed dementia. People who were highly engaged in activity patterns including frequent exercises, household chores, and daily visits of family and friends had 35 percent, 21 percent, and 15 percent lower risk of dementia, respectively, compared with people who were the least engaged in these activity patterns.

Researchers also looked at dementia incidence rates by identified activity patterns. The rate in people who exercised frequently was 0.45 cases for every 1,000 person-years, compared with 1.59 for people who rarely exercised. Those who frequently did household chores had a rate of 0.86 cases for every 1,000 person-years compared with 1.02 for people who rarely did household chores. People who visited friends and family daily had a rate of 0.62 cases for every 1,000 person-years compared with 0.8 cases for those who visited friends and family only once every few months.

Fluctuations in sleep duration may increase the risk of cognitive decline, according to a study presented at the SLEEP 2022 conference. Research on more than 1,100 participants in the long-running Seattle Longitudinal Study (SLS) reported that sleep variability—not simply hours of sleep—predicted risk of cognitive decline over 10 years. For example, researchers explained, the same average seven hours of sleep on paper can be reported by sleepers who slept more hours later in life, those who slept less, and those who maintained a constant number of hours over time. Keeping a constant sleep duration as you age seemed to be key: Increasing sleep variability was consistently associated with worse outcomes at older age.

The Role of Healthy Habits

The overall importance of healthy habits, including diet, was captured in the Chicago Health and Aging Project, a study of 2,449 men and women ages 65 and up. Researchers scored healthy lifestyles based on adherence to the MIND diet, late-life cognitive activities, moderate or vigorous physical activity, non-smoking, and light to moderate alcohol consumption.

Women with four or five healthy lifestyle factors lived 3.1 years longer than those with zero or one; those who developed Alzheimer's spent 10.5 percent of their remaining years with the disease, compared to 19.3 percent for the less-healthy lifestyle group. The healthiest-living women without Alzheimer's enjoyed an average 4.5 extra years. For men, healthy lifestyles were associated with 5.7 extra years (6.4 for those without Alzheimer's), with only 6.1 percent spent with Alzheimer's—half the time of those with zero or one healthy lifestyle factor.

Activity vs. Aging

Among those lifestyle factors, the evidence that physical activity contributes to cognitive health is, if anything, even stronger than the association between nutrition and cognition. As you know, scientific evidence of the cardiovascular benefits of physical activity is overwhelming, and evidence is mounting that physical activity helps protect your brain, too. A randomized trial found that individuals with cognitive impairment saw significant improvements in cognitive executive functioning after six months of walking or cycling for 35 minutes, three times per week.

People who are more physically fit are less likely to develop Alzheimer's disease than people who are less physically fit. In a study of almost 650,000 veterans, initially average age 61, participants were followed for about nine years. They were divided into five fitness levels based on treadmill tests; the fittest group had a level achievable by walking briskly most days of the week, for 150 minutes or more per week. When researchers adjusted for other risk factors, those in the most fit group were 33 percent less likely to develop Alzheimer's disease than those in the least fit group (see "Active Adults Average Bigger Brains").

Activity Against Alzheimer's

Research also shows that greater physical activity levels are associated with slower cognitive decline related to the amyloid compounds that form Alzheimer's brain plaques. In one study, even though there was no association between how much people exercised and amyloid levels, greater activity appeared to affect amyloid's cognitive effects: People who were more active were able to tolerate a higher level of amyloid pathology. Even modest levels of physical activity had notable protective effects, but the greater amyloid tolerance was most prominent in people who took about 8,900 steps a day.

People at a higher genetic risk for Alzheimer's disease might also benefit from physical activity. One study used positron emission tomography (PET) scans to image the brains of people identified as carriers of ApoE epsilon-4, a genetic risk factor for Alzheimer's. Their activity levels were inversely associated with amyloid plaque development in the brain. Among sedentary carriers, the scans showed greater buildup of the plaques associated with Alzheimer's. But the carriers who were physically active showed no more buildup of amyloid plaques than was found in the brains of non-carriers.

Activity vs. Atrophy. Another study reported that people with early Alzheimer's disease who did best on a treadmill test also were less prone to the brain atrophy associated with the disease. The study used the treadmill to measure peak oxygen consumption—a gauge of cardiorespiratory fitness—along with MRI scans to view the brains of patients with early Alzheimer's and a control group of people free of dementia. After the researchers controlled for age, higher peak oxygen consumption was associated with greater whole-brain volume. People with early Alzheimer's disease who were less physically fit had four times more brain shrinkage compared with normal older adults than people who were more physically fit.

How Exercise Helps

One reason physical activity may be associated with protection against dementia is the heart-brain connection. Narrowing of the carotid arteries that lead to the brain may be associated with brain aging and dementia, so good cardiovascular health is good for brain health. Another proposed mechanism is the idea that physical activity increases spatial awareness, which might help support connections in the white matter of the brain. Animal models strongly suggest that physical activity increases certain chemicals in the brain, but it is difficult to study this possibility in humans.

NEW FINDING

Active Adults Average Bigger Brains

Regular exercise seems to build not only bigger muscles but bigger brains as well. A study of 10,125 adults, average age 53, found that those who regularly engaged in moderate to vigorous physical activity had larger average brain volumes. Whole-body MRI scans and multiple brain views were used to assess brain volume. Moderate to vigorous physical activity was defined by activities increasing respiration and pulse rate for at least 10 continuous minutes; three-quarters of participants were active an average of four days per week. Increased days of activity correlated with larger volumes in multiple regions of the brain, including gray matter, white matter, hippocampus, and frontal, parietal, and occipital lobes.

Journal of Alzheimer's Disease, Jan. 16, 2024

NEW FINDING

Sedentary Behavior Linked to Dementia

Based on data from nearly 50,000 adults in the United Kingdom, researchers have shown an association between dementia risk and daily sedentary behavior. Though the study can't prove a causal link, it does support the idea that more time spent not moving—such as sitting while watching TV, working on a computer, or driving—may be a risk factor for dementia. Focusing on adults 60 years and older who wore devices that measure movement, called accelerometers, researchers used machine learning to predict what patterns of accelerometry data predicted sedentary behavior. They then used hospital and death registry data to determine which participants developed dementia in the following years. Median duration of sedentary behavior was just over nine hours per day, similar to results of studies on Americans. The risk for dementia increased greatly for adults who were sedentary more than 10 hours a day.

JAMA, Sept. 12, 2023

The heart-brain connection might be clearest in vascular dementia risk. In an Italian study, regular, non-strenuous physical activity substantially reduced the risk of vascular dementia. Over a four-year span, participants who engaged the most regularly in moderate activity retained the most cognitive function. Regular walking was associated with a 73 percent risk reduction for vascular dementia.

A brisk walk several times a week might also improve the functioning of people already diagnosed with vascular dementia. One study randomly assigned sedentary participants with vascular dementia to a supervised walking program or to a control group. The walkers were asked to move briskly enough to elevate their heart rates to 65 percent of maximum capacity. After six months, the walkers not only had lower blood pressure, but also scored better on cognitive tests and showed less activation in their brains when tackling mental tasks. That is, the walkers' brains seemed to be working more efficiently.

Patients with other cardiovascular health concerns also seem to show brain benefits from exercise. The Women's Antioxidant Cardiovascular Study followed older women who had either prevalent vascular disease or three or more coronary risk factors. The equivalent of a daily brisk 30-minute walk was associated with lower risk of cognitive impairment. As activity levels increased, the rate of cognitive decline decreased..

Other studies have shown that burning as little as an extra 100 calories daily can be enough to move you out of the highest-risk, most sedentary population.

Boosting Brain Volume

Physical activity also seems to affect the brain itself, preserving gray matter and preventing atrophy. Older people who regularly walk, garden, swim, or dance may have bigger brains than their inactive peers. Researchers used magnetic resonance imaging (MRI) scans to measure the brains of people with a range of activity levels. The most active group each week had seven hours of low-intensity physical activity, four hours of moderate physical activity, or two hours of high-intensity physical activity. The scans showed less-active people had smaller brain volume—the equivalent of nearly four years of brain aging (see "Sedentary Behavior Linked to Dementia").

Findings from the Framingham Heart Study also linked extra physical activity—even at a light intensity level—to larger brain volume. In the study of middle-aged adults, every additional hour of light-intensity physical activity per day was associated with greater total brain volume and the equivalent of 1.1 years of less brain aging.

More Gray Matter. Another study assessed activity levels and the volume of gray matter in brain regions typically affected most by Alzheimer's. In a study of almost 900 individuals, initially ages 65 or older, after five years, the most active one-quarter of participants had significantly more gray matter, compared with their most sedentary peers. Greater gray-matter volume, found in parts of the brain associated with memory and higher-level thinking, predicted lower risk of developing mild or severe cognitive impairment (see "Mental Stimulation May Protect the Brain").

Hippocampus Effects. Physical activity seems to specifically benefit hippocampus function, the key part of the inner brain involved in forming, storing, and processing memory. A six-month study using MRI scans of older women who already had mild cognitive impairment found that those assigned to a twice-weekly aerobic walking program saw increases in hippocampal volume.

Getting Going

Becoming more physically active does not have to mean starting a formal, regimented exercise plan. Multiple studies have found that any amount of moderate exercise in otherwise sedentary individuals can reduce the risk of premature death. Analysis of a representative national health survey concluded that an estimated 110,000 deaths a year could be prevented if U.S. adults ages 40 and older increased their moderate-to-vigorous physical activity.

A study of sedentary adults at high risk for developing type 2 diabetes found that simply spending more time standing, rather than sitting, was associated with better insulin sensitivity. In the LIFE (Lifestyle Interventions and Independence for Elders) study, in which Tufts researchers took part, researchers found what is known as a dose-response effect: The more active participants were, the more health benefits were seen. Even a small increase in physical activity led to a reduction in disability.

The Sooner You Start …

Research shows that the sooner you start being active, the better for your brain. The Coronary Artery Risk Development in Young Adults (CARDIA) study reported that the more physically fit you are when you're younger, the more likely you are to keep your brain sharp as you age. Participants, initially ages 18 to 30, walked at an increasingly faster pace on a treadmill until they couldn't continue—an average of 10 minutes. When participants were given cognitive tests 25 years later, each additional minute on the original treadmill measurement was associated with the equivalent of about a year's less mental aging.

That doesn't mean it's too late to get started, even if you were sedentary as a young adult. The small group of participants who improved their fitness from the original treadmill testing scored better on the cognitive assessment than those whose fitness had declined or stayed the same.

Ask your health-care professional for advice about starting an exercise program that's right for you.

Pick Up the Pace

It also pays to pick up your pace. The National Walkers' Health Study, using data on almost 39,000 participants, found that a brisk pace has more benefits than walking slowly—even if the distance traveled is the same. Those reporting a pace slower than a 24-minute mile were at five times greater risk for mortality from dementia. Each additional minute per mile slower in walking pace was associated with a 6.6 percent increased risk of mortality from Alzheimer's disease.

Picking up the pace or frequency of activity can also benefit people who are already experiencing mild cognitive impairment (MCI). Researchers asked 70 sedentary adults diagnosed with MCI to either start a walking regimen or simply do stretching exercises. Frequency increased until, after about six months, participants were working out about five times a week. When participants were retested, the walkers performed better than the stretching group on tests of executive function. Both groups improved their scores on most tests of memory and thinking, however, suggesting that simply getting moving in any way might pay dividends.

Add Strength Training

In addition to aerobic activity, physical-activity guidelines recommend that older people engage in strength training, such as working with weights. Important for fending off frailty, this sort of exercise—sometimes called resistance training—seems to have brain benefits as well.

In a six-month randomized trial of older women suffering from MCI, those

---

NEW FINDING

Mental Stimulation May Protect the Brain

How to exercise your brain? Participating in mentally stimulating activities could help reduce dementia risk among older individuals. A study tracking over 10,000 older Australians found that adult literacy activities (e.g., writing letters or journaling, using a computer, taking education classes) and in active mental activities (e.g., playing games, cards, or chess and doing crosswords or puzzles) was associated with an 11 percent and a 9 percent lower risk of dementia, respectively. Activities like engagement in creative artistic activities and in passive mental activities (reading books, newspapers, or magazines; watching television; and listening to music or the radio) also showed a reduced risk, though to a lesser extent. The findings suggest that keeping the mind active through various activities might contribute to building cognitive reserve, which acts as a buffer against cognitive decline. Surprisingly, social interactions and outings didn't seem to have the same impact on dementia risk in this study, highlighting the specific importance of mentally stimulating activities.

JAMA Network Open, July 14, 2023

We've shared many ways to help boost your brain and heart strength, including exercise, such as walking at a brisk pace.

A Good Night's Sleep

Good sleep habits (sometimes referred to as "sleep hygiene") can help you get a good night's sleep. The Centers for Disease Control and Prevention suggests these habits that can improve your sleep health:

- ☑ **Be consistent.** Go to bed at the same time each night and get up at the same time each morning, including on the weekends.
- ☑ **Make sure your bedroom is quiet,** dark, relaxing, and at a comfortable temperature.
- ☑ **Remove electronic devices,** such as TVs, computers, and smartphones, from the bedroom.
- ☑ **Avoid large meals,** caffeine, and alcohol before bedtime.
- ☑ **Get some exercise.** Being physically active during the day can help you fall asleep more easily at night.

assigned to strength training using machines and free weights significantly improved their scores on memory tests. The study compared strength training versus aerobic exercise (an outdoor walking program) and a control group that did only balance and stretching activities. The aerobic group got fitter but saw no memory benefits. In MRI scans, those in the weight-lifting group also saw significant functional changes in areas of the brain associated with cognition and memory, along with improving their test scores.

Healthy Sleep Habits

Getting a good night's sleep is also important for a healthy heart and brain. In general, good sleepers are less likely to die from cardiovascular causes than those with otherwise healthy lifestyles who don't get adequate sleep. Research links poor sleep with obesity, diabetes, and hypertension. And an observational study published in the *Journal of the American College of Cardiology* found that sleeping fewer hours and having fragmented sleep—defined as frequent awakenings or disruptions in sleep that may be accompanied by difficulty falling back to sleep—promote the buildup of plaque within arteries, which raises the risk of cardiovascular disease independent of other risk factors.

Similarly, the long-running National Health and Aging Trends Study found risk of dementia was double among participants who reported getting less than five hours of sleep compared with those who reported seven to eight hours of sleep per night. Overall, researchers found a strong relationship between several sleep disturbances and deficiency variables and incident dementia over time. Routinely taking 30 minutes or longer to fall asleep was associated with a 45 percent greater risk for incident dementia.

Other studies suggest sleeping too little or too much, abnormal breathing during sleep, and excessive daytime sleepiness are significantly associated with cognitive impairment.

Just-Right Sleep

Like Goldilocks, your brain seems to prefer an amount of sleep that's neither too little nor too much, but just right. That "just right" amount for most people is about seven hours of sleep, give or take an hour or so.

Evidence for this seven-hour sweet spot comes from the large, long-running Nurses' Health Study. Compared with women who slept about seven hours per night, those who slept two hours more or two hours less than seven hours performed worse on cognitive tests. Those sleeping five hours or less and nine hours or more also had beta-amyloid blood markers that predicted a greater risk of cognitive decline and dementia. Overall, abnormal sleep duration was cognitively equivalent to aging by two years.

How to Stick to Healthy Habits

Whether it's eating better or exercising more, adopting healthier habits starts with clarifying your goal. Clearly defined and realistic lifestyle changes that include a specific time frame are more likely to be maintained than vague aspirations. It's not enough to resolve to eat more whole grains or avoid added sugars, for example—be specific.

It is also essential to aim for sustainable behavior change. For example, radical dietary changes may lead to good results in the short term but can be challenging for many to sustain over the long haul. Instead, take sensible, incremental steps toward a healthier overall dietary pattern. Likewise, slowly adding activity beyond your current level is safer (and more effective long-term) than jumping into overly ambitious changes.

Making Time for Change

One roadblock to adopting new, healthier, behaviors—like moving more and cooking healthy meals at home—is finding time to do them. "A new behavior may seem daunting because it's unfamiliar," says Nicole Ninteau, PhD, MPH, adjunct lecturer at Tufts' Friedman School, "but it may turn out to be easier than you think."

Be clear with yourself about what you want to do—and make a plan for how you will do it. Start by setting one or two small, realistic behavior-change goals. "Take a look at your typical routine and consider how any changes will fit in," says Dr. Ninteau. "What are the barriers to making this behavior change, and how can you overcome them?"

If your goal is to be more active, find ways to overcome time-based barriers. Perhaps adding 10 minutes of yoga or stretching to your morning or bedtime routine or a walk at lunch or after dinner would fit your schedule and lifestyle better than a trip to a gym. Since research shows every little bit of movement matters, slip physical activity into your day by doing things like taking the stairs, parking farther from the door, and walking around inside your house for a few minutes during commercials or between episodes of your favorite show. There are many free and low-cost resources online that can provide structure and suggestions for activities that don't require special equipment.

"A lot of successful behavior change comes down to prioritizing the things that will allow you to stick to your plan. Find things you like doing and/or ways to make new behaviors enjoyable," says Dr. Ninteau. "A health behavior we feel like we 'should' do is not the most appealing choice. Try to find things you want to do."

Secrets of Self-Efficacy

"The strongest evidence related to behavior change with regard to diet and physical activity is the idea of self-efficacy," says Sara C. Folta, PhD, who teaches the behavior theory class at Tufts' Friedman School. Simply put, self-efficacy is confidence in your ability to do something. The term was coined by psychologist Albert Bandura in 1977. Research has since linked high self-efficacy to greater ability to deal with adversity and stress, better performance at work or in school, and healthier lifestyle habits.

There are four main areas thought to influence beliefs in our own self-efficacy:

Performance Outcomes. If you have succeeded at something once, you are more likely to believe you can do it again. You may even have the confidence to take on a greater challenge. If you fail, your feelings of self-efficacy can go down. "It's critical to choose appropriate goals," says Dr. Folta. "If, for example, you get winded walking up a flight of stairs, joining a marathon team will reinforce that you cannot be physically active. But if the task is too easy and gives you the sense that anybody can do it, you're not demonstrating to yourself that you can overcome. It might take some trial and error to find the right level for yourself."

Vicarious Experience. "Seeing someone like yourself succeed gives you a sense you can do it, too," says Dr. Folta. "Think about the friends or people in your network who are employing a behavior you strive for. Ask them how they do it. Get their stories of success."

Verbal Persuasion. Encouragement and discouragement influence self-efficacy. If you receive positive feedback, you're

Change Your Habits

Try these tips if you want to change your behavior:

- ☑ **Believe in yourself.** There is strong evidence that confidence in your ability to do something (self-efficacy) is very helpful in changing behaviors around diet and physical activity.
- ☑ **Choose appropriate goals.** Too big a challenge can lower your feelings of self-efficacy. Try something too easy, and you may not build confidence in your abilities.
- ☑ **Look for realistic role models.** Seeing someone like yourself succeed increases confidence that you can do it, too. They may be able to offer some tips or support.
- ☑ **Find a coach.** A supportive friend, family member, or coach can offer encouragement and constructive feedback. A virtual exercise class specific for your energy level can be helpful. Physical activity apps that let you progress at your own pace work for some people.
- ☑ **Don't worry.** Get the knowledge you need to proceed safely, then look at any nervousness as natural, and perhaps even a source of energy. If you are uncertain about a new activity, talk with your health-care provider.
- ☑ **Picture it.** Imagining yourself performing the desired behavior may help you achieve it.

more likely to believe you can succeed. "It's very helpful to have someone who believes in you," says Dr. Folta. Verbal persuasion can also come from a coach. "A good coach will offer encouragement (I know you can do it!)," she explains, "as well as constructive feedback."

Physiological Feedback. Your body's natural response to a stressful situation can create a negative feedback loop. "If trying something new makes you feel a bit anxious, you may feel your heart race," says Dr. Folta. "This can make you more anxious." Instead of interpreting this physiological reaction as a sign that you're not cut out for this new activity or behavior, she suggests you reframe it: "See your racing heart as a sign that you have added energy to infuse into this task. Use it to perform better."

Other Tips. "In addition to believing in your ability to do something and nurturing an environment that encourages your success, taking baby steps is essential to successful behavior change," says Dr. Folta. "For example, rather than deciding to make a massive change to a vegan diet, start by incorporating one new vegetable this week. Do some research and buy one that seems easy to cook and incorporate into dishes or meals you already like. If you don't like the new food, frame it as an information-gathering experience: You learned you don't like that! Each step provides information that helps you determine what to try next."

Start Now

As we've seen throughout this report, you don't have to simply pray for the best and fear the worst when it comes to protecting your heart and brain. You can take proactive steps to improve your odds of healthy aging. By adopting a nutrient-dense dietary pattern, increasing your activity, improving your sleep, and generally committing to a healthier lifestyle, you can increase your odds of living healthier—and mentally sharper—longer.

Why not start today? Your future self will thank you.

10 An Action Plan for a Healthy Lifestyle

Step 1: Know your numbers!

Record your current health statistics from your most recent checkup and check the "Needs Improvement" box to remind you to work on it. (Ask your doctor if you're not sure what your numbers are.)

RISK FACTOR	NUMBER	DATE	GOAL	NEEDS IMPROVEMENT	RECHECK AFTER 6 MOS.	IMPROVED	WORSENED
My blood pressure			Less than 120/Less than 80				
My resting heart rate			A normal resting heart rate for adults ranges from 60 to 100 beats per minute.				
My total cholesterol			Less than 200 mg/dL				
My LDL cholesterol			Less than 100 mg/dL				
My triglycerides			Less than 150 mg/dL				
My BMI (Calculate at https://tinyurl.com/4ntb5dur.)			Less than 25				
My waist/hip ratio (Calculate at https://tinyurl.com/2f4u7nfr.)			0.85 or less for women and 0.9 or less for men				
My fasting blood glucose			Less than 99 mg/dL				
My A1C			Less than 5.7%				

Healthy Heart, Healthy Brain | 67

ACTION PLAN

Blood Pressure

Blood Pressure Categories

CATEGORY	SYSTOLIC MMHG (UPPER NUMBER)		DIASTOLIC MMHG (LOWER NUMBER)
Normal	Less than 120	and	Less than 80
Elevated	120 – 129	and	Less than 80
High Blood Pressure (Stage 1)	130 – 139	or	80 – 89
High Blood Pressure (Stage 2)	140 or higher	or	90 or higher
Hypertensive Crisis (see a doctor)	Higher than 180	and/or	Higher than 120

The American Academy of Family Physicians and American College of Physicians says 140/90 mmHg is the time to start "high" blood pressure treatment.

Blood Sugar

Doctors may check your fasting blood glucose or glycated hemoglobin (HbA1c) level to determine whether you have diabetes or prediabetes.

FASTING BLOOD GLUCOSE LEVEL	CONDITION
70–99 mg/dL	Normal
100–125 mg/dL	Prediabetes
126 mg/dL or higher	Diabetes
HbA1c RESULT	**CONDITION**
Below 5.7%	Normal
5.7% to 6.4%	Prediabetes
6.5% or higher	Diabetes

Cholesterol Numbers

LAB	NORMAL RANGE
Total Cholesterol	125-200 mg/dL
LDL	<100 mg/dL
HDL	Men: 40 mg/dL or higher Women: 50 mg/dL or higher
Triglycerides	<150 mg/dL

A blood test called a lipid panel is used to screen for unhealthy cholesterol levels. The American Heart Association recommends all adults ages 20 or older have their cholesterol checked every four to six years. The National Institutes of Health recommend men ages 45 to 65 and women ages 55 to 65 be screened every one to two years, and adults over 65 be screened annually. A variety of factors must be considered along with cholesterol and triglyceride levels to determine risk of cardiovascular disease. These factors include age, race, lifestyle habits, smoking status, presence of diabetes and/or high blood pressure, and family history. Your doctor also will usually check for high triglycerides as part of a cholesterol test, which is sometimes called a lipid panel or lipid profile. You'll have to fast before blood can be drawn for an accurate triglyceride measurement.

Numbers You Should Know

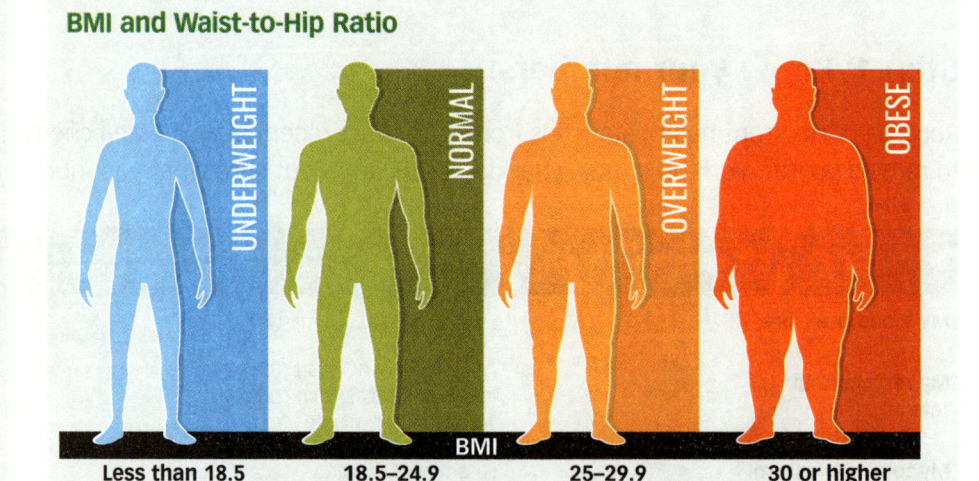

BMI and Waist-to-Hip Ratio

UNDERWEIGHT	NORMAL	OVERWEIGHT	OBESE
Less than 18.5	18.5–24.9	25–29.9	30 or higher

BMI

Body Mass Index (BMI) is a measure of body fat based on height and weight that applies to adult men and women. Note: You may read that the BMI system is flawed because it doesn't account for things like age, gender, fitness, and so on. While we wait for science to make a determination, the BMI is a good index. If you have questions, discuss the findings with your health-care provider.

To find out your BMI, use the online BMI calculator at the National Heart, Lung, and Blood Institute's website: https://bit.ly/39dXVKV.

Waist-to-hip ratio is another factor sometimes used in predicting cardiovascular risk. To calculate your ratio, divide your waist measurement by your hip measurement. For example, a person with a 36-inch waist and a 38-inch hip circumference would have a ratio of 0.95. The World Health Organization advises that a healthy waist-hip ratio is 0.85 or less for women and 0.9 or less for men.

Guidelines from this Special Health Report

Recheck your numbers after six months of following these recommendations.

Understand Dementia

- **Most episodes of everyday forgetfulness are normal;** if you're not sure, consult your physician.
- **Clear scientific evidence shows that your everyday dietary choices** can make a big difference in your brain health.
- **The fact that severe dementia can cause you to lose your normal life,** be unable to recognize family and friends, or even understand them should be enough to motivate you to take charge now.

The Heart-Brain Connection

- **Learn the warning signs of stroke: FAST (Face, Arm, Speech, Time to dial 911).** The sooner treatment is administered, the better the outcome.
- **Get your health under control.** A high resting heart rate is a risk factor for stroke.
- **What is a healthy diet?** Healthy eating helps keep your heart and brain functioning well. Include whole foods, nuts, seeds, fruits, and vegetables, and cook using a healthy oil, like olive oil.
- **What are the best vegetables to eat, or the best brain foods?** There's no single "best" in heart-healthy meals or eating for brain health. Choose nutritious foods like those in healthy dietary patterns; prepare them simply without excess sodium, sugar, or caloric sauces; and focus on minimally processed foods you enjoy.
- **Limit saturated fat,** like red meats, butter and stick margarine, cheese, pastries and sweets, fried foods, and fast foods.
- **Practice healthy eating habits by following a healthy dietary pattern** such as the Mediterranean, DASH, or MIND plans.
- **Be wary of fad diets.** An overall healthy dietary pattern makes the difference, not just popping a few healthy foods.

Nutrients You Need

- **Carbohydrates are not a dietary no-no,** as carbs provide energy for the body, especially the brain and the nervous system.
- **Nutritious foods, such as fruits, vegetables, milk, and other dairy products,** provide essential vitamins and minerals.
- **Multiple studies have found cardiovascular benefits from adopting a vegetarian or mostly vegetarian diet.** Even if you don't go that far, opt for "meatless Monday" or otherwise plan one or two plant-based meals weekly.
- **Keep up your fatty-acid intake.** High blood levels of DHA have been linked to a reduced risk of dementia and Alzheimer's disease.
- **The AHA recommends eating fish at least two times a week;** one serving is 3.5 ounces cooked, or about three-quarters of a cup of flaked fish. Choose varieties higher in omega-3s and less prone to contaminants.

- **Stay hydrated,** but don't stress over rules about water consumption. Fluid needs depend upon many factors: body size, physical activity level, ambient temperature, humidity, and even altitude.
- **Coffee and tea "count" toward your fluid needs** and may even have plant-like health benefits. Avoid lattes and drinks with added sugar and saturated fats, however.
- **Drink alcohol only in moderation,** if at all.
- **Talk to your doctor about supplements,** but don't expect the same results you will get from nutritious, natural food.
- **Be especially wary of infomercials** and those long TV ad programs pushing one supplement or another. If they worked, why would they have to spend so much money pushing them?

Lifestyle Habits

- **Research shows that, as people's fitness improved,** their risk of Alzheimer's disease decreased.
- **Physical activity increases blood flow to the brain,** boosting brain power and reducing the risk for vascular dementia.
- **Aim to move more and sit less throughout the day.** Some physical activity is better than none. Adults who sit less and do any amount of moderate-to- vigorous physical activity gain some health benefits.
- **For substantial health benefits,** adults should do at least 150 minutes (2 hours and 30 minutes) to 300 minutes (5 hours) a week of moderate-intensity, or 75 minutes (1 hour and 15 minutes) to 150 minutes (2 hours and 30 minutes) a week of vigorous-intensity aerobic physical activity, or an equivalent combination of moderate- and vigorous-intensity aerobic activity. Preferably, aerobic activity should be spread throughout the week.
- **Additional health benefits are gained by engaging in physical activity beyond the equivalent of 300 minutes** (5 hours) of moderate-intensity physical activity a week.
- **Adults should also do muscle-strengthening activities of moderate or greater intensity and that involve all major muscle groups on 2 or more days a week,** as these activities provide additional health benefits.
- **Don't forget the importance of a good night's sleep.** See tips on page 64.
- **How to improve mental agility?** How to increase brain power? Research shows that building a "cognitive reserve" can keep your brain youthful. Besides physical activity, regular mental activity—games, puzzles, writing and reading, even crafting—contributes to a healthy brain.

After six months of following these tips and the advice in this Special Report, recheck your key health numbers. If you haven't seen improvement, or the numbers worsened, contact your physician for more ways to improve your numbers.

If they did improve, congratulations! You're well on your way to a healthy heart and healthy brain!

RECIPES

Banana Walnut Muffins

Ingredients

- 3 over-ripe bananas
- 2 large eggs
- 2 cups whole-wheat pastry flour (or white whole-wheat flour)
- ⅓ cup sugar
- 1 tsp salt
- 1 tsp baking soda
- ½ cup chopped walnuts

Steps

1. Preheat oven to 350°F and lightly grease and flour 10 cups of a muffin tin.
2. Mix bananas and eggs together thoroughly with an electric mixer.
3. Sift dry ingredients (flour, sugar, salt, baking soda) together. Add to bananas and eggs.
4. Add nuts while mixing just until everything is combined. (Overmixing makes muffins dense.)
5. Spoon into muffin tins, filling each cup about ¾ full.
6. Bake for 20 minutes; muffins are done if a toothpick comes out clean. Cook a few minutes longer if toothpick comes out wet and sticky.

YIELD: 10 Muffins
PER SERVING (1 MUFFIN): 192 calories, 6 g total fat, 1 g sat fat, 6 g protein, 33 g carbs, 4 g fiber, 375 mg sodium
SOURCE: Oldways Whole Grains Council (wholegrainscouncil.org)

Weight and Measure Abbreviations

oz = ounce
tsp = teaspoon
Tbsp = tablespoon
lb = pound
g = gram
mg = milligram

Healthy Heart, Healthy Brain

Cupboard Minestrone Soup

Ingredients

- 3 cups water
- 1 medium diced onion
- 2 medium sliced carrots
- 2 cloves minced garlic
- 1 (10.75 oz) can low sodium tomato soup, condensed
- 1 (14.5 oz) can cut green beans, with liquid
- 1 (15 oz) sweet corn, with liquid
- 1 cup whole grain elbow macaroni, uncooked
- 1 Tbsp Italian seasoning (or dried oregano)
- 1 tsp black pepper

Steps

1. Heat water in a large pot.
2. Add onion, carrots, and garlic. Cover with a lid and cook for 10 minutes.
3. Add tomato soup, green beans with liquid, corn with liquid, white beans with liquid, macaroni, Italian seasoning, and black pepper.
4. Cook for 15 to 20 minutes, covered, stirring occasionally, until pasta is tender.
5. Serve immediately.

YIELD: 8 servings (1½ cups each)
PER SERVING: 219 calories, 1 g total fat, 0 g sat fat, 10 g protein, 46 g carbs, 8 g fiber, 10 g sugar, 324 mg sodium
SOURCE: Recipe and photo courtesy of Sharon Palmer for Tomato Products Wellness Council

Alice's Homemade Pita Chips

Ingredients
3 whole pitas
1½ Tbsp plant oil (like canola or safflower) or spray oil
Toppings of your choosing (such as garlic powder, chili powder, oregano, or sesame seeds)

Steps
1. Preheat oven to 400°F.
2. Split pitas and cut rounds into triangles. Spread triangles on a baking sheet.
3. Brush or spray both sides lightly with oil.
4. Sprinkle with herbs and/or spices, if desired
5. Bake 5 to 10 minutes, until crisp and beginning to brown. (Keep a close eye, as they burn quickly.) For even crispness, flip halfway through cooking.

YIELD: 6 servings
PER SERVING: 101 calories, 4 g total fat, 0 g sat fat, 1 g protein, 13 g carbs, 2 g fiber, 1 g sugar, 155 mg sodium
SOURCE: Recipe: *Tufts Health & Nutrition Letter*; Image: © Brian Macdonald | Getty Images

Savory Roasted Papaya and Pineapple Side Dish

Ingredients

- 1 papaya (about 2 cups cubed)
- 1 pineapple (about 4 cups cubed)
- 2 Tbsp olive oil
- 2 Tbsp, or 2 tsp dried fresh tarragon
- 1 Tbsp fresh or 2 tsp dried thyme
- 1 tsp salt
- 1 tsp black pepper

Steps

1. Preheat oven to 375°F.
2. Peel papaya, scoop out seeds, and cube into one-inch chunks.
3. Peel pineapple, core, and cut into one-inch chunks.
4. In a large bowl, toss fruit with olive oil, herbs, salt, and pepper.
5. Spread fruit out on a baking dish and cook until tops of fruit begin to brown, about 20 minutes.
6. Turn oven up to 425°F and cook until fruit edges caramelize, about 8 to 10 minutes.
7. Remove from oven and serve.

YIELD: 6 servings
PER SERVING: 118 calories, 5 g total fat, 1 g sat fat, 3 g protein, 20 g carbs, 3 g fiber, 15 g sugar, 393 mg sodium
SOURCE: Recipe adapted courtesy Melissa's Produce www.melissas.com

Roasted Salmon with North African Herb Sauce

Ingredients

- ¼ cup chopped fresh parsley
- ¼ cup chopped fresh cilantro (or another ¼ cup parsley)
- 2 cloves medium cloves garlic, minced
- 1 tsp paprika
- 1 tsp ground cumin
- Pinch of ground red pepper (cayenne)
- ⅛ tsp salt
- Pepper to taste
- ¼ cup nonfat plain yogurt
- 2 Tbsp lemon juice, plus wedges for serving
- 1 Tbsp vegetable oil
- 1⅛ lb salmon fillet, cut into 4 portions

Steps

1. Stir together parsley, cilantro, garlic, paprika, cumin, ground red pepper, salt, and pepper in small bowl. Add yogurt, lemon juice, and oil; mix well. Reserve 1/3 cup for sauce; set aside, covered, in the refrigerator.
2. Place fish on plate. Rub remaining parsley mixture over fish. Cover and marinate in the refrigerator for at least 20 minutes or up to 1 hour.
3. Meanwhile, preheat oven to 400ºF. Line a small baking sheet or baking pan with aluminum foil. Coat foil with cooking spray.
4. Transfer fish to prepared baking sheet. Bake until fish flesh is opaque and begins to flake, 12 to 20 minutes, depending on thickness. Serve fish with lemon wedges, vegetable, and choice of grain dish.

YIELD: 4 (3-oz) servings
PER SERVING: 230 calories, 12 g total fat, 2 g sat fat, 27 g protein, 3 g carbs, 1 g fiber, 1 g sugar, 140 mg sodium
SOURCE: *Tufts Health & Nutrition Letter*

Easy Peach Crisp

Ingredients
- 1 tsp unsalted butter
- ½ cup rolled oats
- 1 tsp sugar
- ¼ tsp cinnamon
- 1 Tbsp olive oil
- 2 cups peaches, diced (or apples, berries, etc.)
- Optional for serving: vanilla frozen yogurt

Steps
1. Preheat oven to 350°F. Grease a 6 ½-inch cast iron skillet with butter.
2. In a small bowl, toss the oats with the cinnamon, sugar, and olive oil.
3. Put the fruit in the skillet, then top with the oat mixture. Bake for 35 minutes, until fruit is bubbly and oats are golden.
4. Let cool for 5 to 10 minutes, then top with a scoop of vanilla frozen yogurt, if desired. (Caution: Skillet will be very hot.)

YIELD: 2 servings
PER SERVING, WITHOUT YOGURT: 209 calories, 11 g total fat, 2 g sat fat, 6 g protein, 34 g carbs, 6 g fiber, 14 g sugar, 1 mg sodium
SOURCE: Oldways, www.oldwayspt.org

OTHER MEAL IDEAS

More Breakfast Ideas

- Plain yogurt mixed with berries, low-calorie granola or nuts, cinnamon, and a drizzle of honey
- Whole-grain cereal with berries or sliced bananas
- Whole-wheat toast or English muffin with nut butter and sliced bananas
- Oatmeal (preferably steel-cut) with berries or dried fruits, cinnamon, and nuts
- Whole-wheat breakfast burrito with a mix of eggs and egg whites, cheese, beans and salsa

More Lunch Ideas

- Nut butter sandwich on whole-wheat bread, with a piece of fruit and small yogurt
- Veggie "burger" on whole-wheat hamburger bun, with lettuce and tomato; fruit or yogurt for dessert
- Egg sandwich (1 large boiled egg, mixed and mashed with ¾ Tbsp Dijon mustard, served on 2 slices whole-wheat bread); serve with lightly dressed lettuce salad and a piece of fruit
- Half a boneless, skinless chicken breast, grilled or sautéed in a little olive oil (season chicken with your choice of no-salt Italian seasoning, chili powder, or Cajun seasoning), served on whole-wheat hamburger bun with lettuce and tomato; fruit or yogurt for dessert
- Two eggs (scrambled, poached, or fried in a little olive oil), whole-wheat toast, with side of fresh tomatoes or avocado
- Small salmon fillet, grilled or sautéed in a little olive oil, served with half-portion of whole-grain pasta (such as rotini) tossed and topped with jarred pesto
- Tuna-salad sandwich made with canned (or pouch) tuna in water, Greek yogurt, chopped celery, and chives, on whole-wheat bread

More Snack Ideas

- Slice of whole-wheat toast or English muffin with nut butter
- Small yogurt with ½ cup whole-grain cereal or berries
- Half-cup cottage cheese and small peach
- Half-cup unsweetened applesauce
- 4 stalks celery spread with 2 Tbsp peanut butter
- ¼ cup cottage cheese mixed with 2 Tbsp jarred salsa; 10 baby carrots and 6 whole-grain crackers for dipping
- 1 oz part-skim mozzarella cheese stick with 2 oz whole-grain pretzels
- 1 cup air-popped popcorn

More Dinner Ideas

- Fish tacos made from your favorite flaky fish (broiled, grilled, sautéed in a little oil, baked without breading, or poached), corn tortillas, lettuce, tomato, avocado, and low-sodium taco sauce.
- Simple stir fry with 3 oz chicken per serving, seasonal vegetables, low-sodium soy sauce, grated ginger, garlic, and red pepper flakes to taste. Serve with brown rice.
- Grilled shrimp or grilled and sliced chicken breast, served atop your favorite salad mix (see vinaigrette recipe below), with a handful of your favorite nuts instead of croutons.

More Side Dish Ideas

- Whole grains such as brown rice, farro, barley, or quinoa, prepared according to package directions. To serve risotto style, sauté half an onion in olive oil, then add grain and stir until lightly toasted; add warm low-sodium chicken stock a half-cup at a time, stirring and waiting until liquid is almost all absorbed before adding more, and until grains are tender; top with a little parmesan cheese.
- Sweet potatoes, baked whole or cut into bite-size pieces, tossed with olive oil and paprika, and roasted.
- Whole-grain pasta, prepared according to package directions and tossed with a little olive oil.
- Seasonal vegetables, steamed, microwaved, or lightly sautéed. Add flavor with lemon juice or a dash of spices.
- Canned beans, drained and rinsed, or fat-free refried beans.
- Frozen peas, lima beans, or vegetable mix, prepared according to package directions.
- Lettuce salad tossed with a simple vinaigrette: Whisk together 2 Tbsp vinegar, ½ to 1 tsp Dijon-style mustard, ¼ tsp kosher salt, ¼ tsp freshly ground black pepper, 6 Tbsp extra-virgin olive oil (or other vegetable oil), adding the oil in a stream. Vary vinaigrette by adding 2 Tbsp finely chopped shallots or fresh herbs, a dash of onion or garlic powder or dried herbs, or trying various types of vinegar.

More Dessert Ideas

- 1 cup diced melon
- Quick pineapple shake: Blend ½ cup fresh pineapple, ¼ cup plain nonfat yogurt, 1 Tbsp honey, 1 cup skim milk, 10 ice cubes per serving.
- 1 cup berries topped with ½ cup nonfat Greek yogurt, 1 Tbsp dark chocolate chips
- ½ cup tapioca pudding with 1 Tbsp walnuts

GLOSSARY

added sugars: Sugars that are added to foods or beverages when they are processed or prepared. Naturally occurring sugars such as those in fruit or milk are not added sugars.

Alzheimer's disease: A progressive, irreversible, and incurable form of dementia involving deterioration of brain tissue that leads to memory loss, personality changes, and other mental impairment. It is the most common form of dementia and affects more than 6 million people in the United States. (See: Dementia)

angina: Chest pain caused by inadequate blood supply to the heart.

antioxidants: Substances in the blood that protect cells from damage caused by free radicals—harmful unstable molecules produced in normal chemical reactions or in response to stress or exposure to environmental toxins. Antioxidants include flavonoids, beta-carotene, lycopene, selenium, and vitamins A, C, and E. Many more compounds in fruits, vegetables, legumes, nuts, and whole grains act as antioxidants.

artery: A major blood vessel that supplies oxygen-rich blood to the body's tissues.

bioactive compounds: Substances that have actions in the body that may promote good health.

carbohydrates: Compounds of carbon, hydrogen, and oxygen that form sugars, starches, and cellulose. Carbohydrates are one of the body's main sources of energy.

cardiovascular disease: Conditions that affect the heart and blood vessels, including coronary artery disease, myocardial infarction (heart attack), stroke, heart failure, arrhythmia, peripheral artery disease, deep vein thrombosis, pulmonary embolism, and cardiomyopathy.

cholesterol: A waxy, fat-like substance found in foods of animal origin and synthesized by the body that can contribute to cardiovascular disease. In the blood, serum cholesterol combines with proteins to form LDL and HDL cholesterol. Serum cholesterol can contribute to plaque buildup in the arteries.

cognition: Conscious intellectual activity, such as thinking and memory, orientation, language, judgment, and problem-solving.

cognitive decline: A loss of cognitive function, such as that associated with dementia.

coronary artery disease (CAD): A condition caused by the buildup of fatty plaques in the artery walls, which narrows the blood vessels and prevents enough oxygen from reaching the heart.

DASH diet: The Dietary Approaches to Stop Hypertension eating plan is high in fruits, vegetables, grains, and other plant foods, and low in meat, sweets, and salt. This diet was designed to decrease blood pressure; it is low in saturated fat, total fat, and cholesterol.

dementia: A progressive illness that results in memory loss and other cognitive abnormalities that over time seriously interfere with daily life. There are several forms of dementia, the most common of which is Alzheimer's disease.

diabetes: a disease in which the body's ability to produce or respond to the hormone insulin is impaired. This results in abnormal metabolism of carbohydrates and elevated levels of glucose (blood sugar).

dietary pattern: The quantity, variety, or combination of different foods and beverages and the frequency with which they are consumed.

docosahexaenoic acid (DHA): A type of omega-3 fatty acid found in fish that is essential for heart and brain health.

eicosapentaenoic acid (EPA): A type of omega-3 fatty acid found in fish that is essential for heart and brain health.

fats: Compounds containing fatty acids, which may be monounsaturated, polyunsaturated, or saturated.

fatty acids: The building blocks of fats. They take the form of chains of different lengths that may be straight (saturated) or bent (unsaturated).

fiber: dietary material that cannot be broken down through digestion.

flavonoids: A group of more than 5,000 antioxidant compounds naturally present in vegetables, fruits, and beverages like tea, red wine, and fruit juices. Research suggests flavonoids may protect against damage to blood vessels, decreasing the risk of cardiovascular disease. In addition, they may have a role in cancer prevention and may help boost the immune system.

hemorrhagic stroke: A stroke caused by a weakened blood vessel in the brain that ruptures and bleeds.

high-density lipoprotein (HDL) cholesterol: Often referred to as "good" cholesterol, HDL cholesterol reduces cholesterol buildup in the arteries, thereby reducing the risk of heart disease.

hypertension: High blood pressure. Known as "the silent killer," hypertension is a very important risk factor for stroke and heart attack as well as other disorders.

insulin resistance: Reduced sensitivity to insulin that is typical of type 2 diabetes, but also may occur in the absence of diabetes.

insulin: A hormone released by the pancreas that causes cells to take up sugar (glucose) from the bloodstream to use and store for energy. Insulin is important in carbohydrates, fat, and protein metabolism.

legumes: A seed, pod, or other edible part of various plants in the pea family, including lentils, peas, chickpeas, beans, soybeans, and peanuts.

lipids: Fats or fat-like substances. Lipid levels in the bloodstream are commonly measured to evaluate cardiovascular health risks. Lipids include LDL cholesterol, HDL cholesterol, and triglycerides.

lipoprotein: A spherical particle in the blood composed of protein and lipids. Its role is to move lipids from one part of the body to another.

low-density lipoprotein (LDL) cholesterol: Often referred to as "bad" cholesterol, LDL transports cholesterol to the arteries, where it can build up and lead to heart disease. It contains more fat and less protein than HDL. LDL invades artery walls and contributes to plaque buildup, leading to clogged arteries and cardiovascular disease.

lycopene: The natural red pigment that gives tomatoes their color. Research suggests it is a powerful antioxidant that may have health benefits. Most of the lycopene in the diet comes from cooked tomato products such as canned tomatoes, spaghetti sauce, and ketchup.

macronutrients: The nutrients we need in larger quantities that provide energy (calories). Fat, protein, and carbohydrates are the three macronutrients.

Mediterranean-style diet: A dietary style based on traditional dietary patterns of Mediterranean countries, particularly Italy, Greece, and Spain. It emphasizes olive oil as the primary source of dietary fat, an abundance of plant foods, including fruits and vegetables, whole grains, beans, nuts, and seeds, and moderate amounts of fish, poultry, cheese, and yogurt.

micronutrients: Essential nutrients we need in very small amounts. Includes vitamins and minerals.

mild cognitive impairment (MCI): A decline in mental functions such as memory and decision-making that is not severe enough to interfere with daily activities.

monounsaturated fat: A type of healthy fat in which one carbon atom is not bound to hydrogen; monounsaturated fats, found in olive, walnut, canola, and other vegetable oils, are generally liquid at room temperature.

omega-3 fatty acids: Essential fatty acids found in fish, walnuts, soy products, and some seeds and vegetable oils that can reduce the risk of cardiovascular disease and may help protect brain function.

omega-6 fatty acids: A type of unsaturated fat found in many nuts, seeds, and vegetable oils, and in some poultry, seafood, and vegetables. One omega-6 fatty acid, linoleic acid, is essential to the body.

phytochemicals (also called phytonutrients): Compounds in plants that provide flavor, aroma, and color, and protect the plant from microbes and environmental damage. When consumed by humans, phytochemicals may promote health and prevent disease. Many phytochemicals have antioxidant properties.

plaque: A build-up of cholesterol and other substances that narrows arteries.

polyphenols: A group of naturally occurring plant compounds, including flavonoids and isoflavones, with antioxidant properties that may benefit health.

polyunsaturated fat: A type of fat in which more than one carbon atom is not bound to hydrogen; polyunsaturated fats are healthy and generally liquid at room temperature, as in vegetable oil.

protein: Essential constituents of living cells; plants or animal tissues that contain protein supply essential amino acids to the body.

saturated fat: A type of fat that can increase unhealthy cholesterol levels and raise the risk of heart disease. Saturated fatty acids are found primarily in animal foods, especially meats and full-fat dairy products.

soluble fiber: A type of fiber that attracts water into the bowel and forms a gel during digestion. Viscous soluble fiber may help lower blood cholesterol levels.

thrombus: A blood clot that forms in the vascular system and blocks blood flow.

trans fat: A type of fat in processed foods that is manufactured by adding hydrogen to liquid oil to solidify it, resulting in the formation of a partially hydrogenated oil. Trans fat increases unhealthy LDL cholesterol levels and lowers healthy HDL cholesterol levels. Note: Trans fats were banned by the U.S. Food & Drug Administration in 2018.

transient ischemic attack (TIA): Also known as a "mini-stroke," a TIA is a stroke that lasts only a few minutes, briefly interrupting blood flow to part of the brain.

triglycerides: Three fatty acids attached to a glycerol backbone; they serve as the main storage unit for excess calories.

unsaturated fat: A type of fatty acid that lowers cholesterol levels and reduces the risk for coronary artery disease when it is consumed in place of saturated fats. Monounsaturated and polyunsaturated fatty acids fall into this category.

vascular dementia: Dementia caused by blood vessel damage in the brain, the second-most common form of dementia after Alzheimer's disease.

RESOURCES

Academy of Nutrition and Dietetics
eatright.org

Alzheimer's Association
alz.org

Alzheimer's Drug Discovery Foundation
alzdiscovery.org

Alzheimer's Foundation of America
alzfdn.org

American Academy of Sleep Medicine
SleepEducation.org

American Diabetes Association
diabetes.org

American Heart Association
heart.org

American Institute for Cancer Research
aicr.org

Association for Frontotemporal Degeneration (AFTD)
theaftd.org

Caregiver Action Network
caregiveraction.org

Centers for Disease Control and Prevention (CDC)
cdc.gov

Dietary Guidelines for Americans
dietaryguidelines.gov

Friedman School of Nutrition Science and Policy—Tufts University
nutrition.tufts.edu

Jean Mayer USDA Human Nutrition Research Center on Aging
hnrca.tufts.edu

Lewy Body Dementia Association
www.lbda.org

National Council on Aging
ncoa.org

National Heart, Lung, and Blood Institute (NHLBI)
nhlbi.nih.gov

National Institute of Mental Health (NIMH)
nimh.nih.gov

National Institute of Neurological Disorders and Stroke
www.ninds.nih.gov

National Institute on Aging Alzheimer's Disease Education and Referral Center
nia.nih.gov/alzheimers

Office of Nutrition and Health Promotion Programs (ONHPP)
acl.gov

Oldways Whole Grains Council
wholegrainscouncil.org

Physical Activity Guidelines for Americans
health.gov/paguidelines

Tufts Health & Nutrition Letter
nutritionletter.tufts.edu

Tufts' MyPlate for Older Adults
hnrca.tufts.edu/myplate

U.S. Department of Agriculture (USDA) Choose My Plate
choosemyplate.gov